THE SCREENWRITING

Sensei

A COMPLETE GUIDE TO WRITING YOUR FIRST SCRIPT

BY

PAUL CHITLIK

MICHAEL WIESE PRODUCTIONS

Published by Michael Wiese Productions
12400 Ventura Blvd. #1111
Studio City, CA 91604
(818) 379-8799, (818) 986-3408 (FAX)
mw@mwp.com
www.mwp.com

Cover design by Johnny Ink
Back cover photo by John Salcedo, L.A. City Films
Interior design by William Morosi
Copyediting by Karen Krumpak

Manufactured in the United States of America

First Printing 2025

FSC
www.fsc.org
MIX
Paper | Supporting responsible forestry
FSC® C008955

PRAISE FOR THE SCREENWRITING SENSEI

"Breezy, accessible, well-conceived. Less a writing primer and more a personal tutorial, it effortlessly guides the reader through the crea"tion of the first draft of a screenplay. What could be more valuable to a writer? Few books match its combination of clarity and usefulness."

—**Dana Coen**, executive producer of *JAG* and *Bones* and director of the Writing for the Screen and Stage program at the University of North Carolina, Chapel Hill

"An entire screenwriting course in one entertaining volume by a true sensei of the craft. Paul's valuable lessons and wisdom deserve a place in every screenwriting classroom and aspiring writer's bookshelf."

—**Brian Price**, screenwriting professor and author of *Classical Storytelling and Contemporary Screenwriting*

"Many people have great ideas and great talent but fail to write out of one thing—fear; fear that they don't understand the process, fear that they don't understand the industry. The lessons that Paul Chitlik first taught me in his class—lessons in this book—removed that fear. In the place of fear, creativity and productivity were able to take root."

—**Sarah Nicole Jones**, executive producer of *Waco* and *Altered Carbon*

"There are dozens of Hollywood screenwriters wishing Paul would stop giving away all their secrets. Read this book before they find a way to stop him."

—**Jay Douglas**, author of *I Don't Have All the Answers Only Because There Are Too Many Questions*

"The fourth book I read on screenwriting, the first one that made the entire process more approachable and less abstract. The author's personality was quite consciously part of the narrative. Like listening to a friend talking me through how to write a screenplay."

—**Neal Howe**, former CABLE TV company CEO and aspiring screenwriter

"I've been a writer in Hollywood for forty-five years (Yikes!), won lots of writing awards, and trust me, Paul Chitlik is a master at delineating the film-writing process. His most sage advice in a book full of sage advice: Writers write. If you have a passion for writing (and rewriting) screenplays and more than your average reserve of stick-to-itiveness, this is an excellent starting point. Good luck!"

—**Allen Rucker**, author of *The Sopranos: A Family History*, cowriter of the WGA Award–winning *The History of White People in America*, and writer of *Hometown Boy Makes Good*

"Paul's new book is an invaluable resource for aspiring screenwriters and a powerful refresher course for professionals across all genres. Each chapter builds on Paul's decades of experience as a professor and successful screenwriter, and his guidance and insights are constructive, informative, accessible, and inspiring. It's an exciting and essential text, and I'm adding it to my course syllabus STAT!"

—**Neil Landau**, screenwriting professor at the University of Georgia; writer of *Don't Tell Mom the Babysitter's Dead*, and writer for *Melrose Place, The Magnificent Seven, Doogie Howser, M.D., The Secret World of Alex Mack*, and MTV's *Undressed*; and executive producer of Goya Award–winning *Tad: The Lost Explorer, Mummies*, and *Buffalo Kids*

"Paul proves it: A screenwriting guide can also be a fun read! As a kids' animation writer, I plan to keep *The Screenwriting Sense*i near me while I write my next episode. The references are both modern and timeless; writers of any age will benefit from this book."

—**Eden Russo**, writer for Nickelodeon's *Wylde Pak*

"Few books explore screenwriting as effectively as this one. Engaging and insightful, it's a must read for both aspiring and experienced writers. I highly recommend this book—not just for students, but also for screenwriting teachers seeking a deeper, more structured approach to the craft."

—**Jenő Hódi**, director of the Budapest Film Academy, American-Hungarian, and multiple award–winning director, writer, and producer

"Writing a great screenplay is freakin' hard. Anyone who says otherwise has never written one. *The Screenwriting Sensei* offers a master class in making the journey a little easier and a lot less mysterious."

—**Star Frohman**, Scott Newman Award–winning writer of *Beverly Hills, 90210, Any Day Now, Early Edition, Life Goes On,* and *Twice in a Lifetime*

"Everyone has a story to tell and right to do so. Paul Chitlik's *Screenwriting Sensei* provides an entertaining roadmap to share those stories through advice, exercises, and insights."

—**Doug Neil**, former Universal Pictures executive vice president of digital marketing; chief digital officer at Freedom Forum

"Home run! This book doesn't rely on gimmicky tricks that regurgitate the same old Hollywood talking points on writing screenplays. It's an authentic take on writing—from the perspective of someone who has been there. Truly a pleasure to read. A must for every screenwriter—new or experienced."

—**Carlo P.A. Dall'Olmo**, president of the Phoenix Screenwriters Association

"Paul's easily digested and accessible methods have, without question, assisted me in every aspect of every step in my storytelling. Whether outlining, writing, or rewriting, I find myself referring to my notes from almost fifteen years ago to get me started, get me moving, or get me out of a jam."

—**Robert Brickman**, graduate of the AFI MFA program in Screenwriting

"As a career diplomat, I've learned that you need to listen to all kinds of people to get the real story on the ground. People have really good reasons for what they do. Chitlik says the same about creating characters. Even more importantly, he believes you have to have a premise—a unifying theme in what you write. This book helped me find the unifying theme of my work as I write the memoir of my years at USAID."

—**Andrew Sisson**, USAID former mission director for East Africa, Pakistan, Indonesia, and others

"In *The Screenwriting Sensei*, Paul Chitlik takes aspiring writers on a journey that starts with the dreaded blank page and ends with a first draft screenplay. With hard facts and gentle encouragement, wisdom and humor, insight and inspiration, his roadmap is at once simple and savvy—easy to navigate while rich with his long experience in the field. Maybe best of all, Paul's voice is a comfortable one: Newcomers will feel like he's talking just to them, and is dedicated to their success. Just like the best senseis are."

—**Mary McDonald-Lewis**, writer, director, and dialect coach, and actor in *Lightyear, G.I. Joe, Grimm,* and others

"'Sensei' Chitlik outlines the key elements of powerful storytelling underpinning every successful project whether on the screen or the page. A valuable foundational guide for the screenwriter's work."

—**Linda Moore**, author of award-winning novel *Five Days in Bogota*

"Whether you're struggling with your first script or diving into rewrites on your fifteenth, Paul Chitlik's valuable lessons will help you strengthen your story before it gets into the hands of Hollywood gatekeepers. Learn from Paul—like so many successful UCLA students have—and give your dream of becoming a working screenwriter a fighting chance."

—**Brian Fagan**, director of the UCLA School of Theater, Film, and Television's Professional Programs

"I've been writing TV and screenplays professionally for fifty years. Despite all I know and all I've done, I never hand in any work until Paul Chitlik says it's ready. He is my final arbiter. Enough said."

—**Marc Sheffler**, writer for *Harry and the Hendersons, Charles in Charge, Who's the Boss?,* and *People's Choice Awards*

For Jody Wheeler,
Student, colleague, collaborator, friend

CONTENTS

Course 1

INTRODUCTION TO SCREENWRITING I

Course 2
SCREENWRITING II: WORKS IN PROGRESS

Course 3
INTRODUCTION TO SCREENWRITING III

INTRODUCTION TO THE INTRODUCTION

The lectures and assignments in this book are taken directly from courses I taught online at UCLA Extension in the early 2000s. At that time, online courses were taught asynchronously. Students could log in at any time to read the lectures and do the work. They were also required to post their biographies, their homework, and their thoughts on other students' work, so we developed a writers room for each class, much the same way as we did in brick-and-mortar classrooms where I also taught in UCLA Extension's Writers' Program, UCLA'S Professional Program in Screenwriting, UCLA'S MFA program in Screenwriting, and later as a clinical associate professor at Loyola Marymount University. I also would comment on their work in either public or private spaces depending on whether the comments would benefit the individual or the class as a whole. Unfortunately, I can't do that in this book.

But this book will take you on the same journey to write a full-length filmscript. And if you can round up a writers group, there is some guidance as how to help each other out in discussions of your work.

I noticed as I reviewed the lectures that many from the first course were repeated in the second and third courses. This made sense at the time since it was rare that students followed me from one course to another or that I even taught the courses in sequence. So I have either removed repeated lectures or have emphasized parts of them to refresh your memory as you tackle the more challenging issues in screenwriting. I've then inserted lectures from other courses, such as my lectures "Deep Structure" and "Watching Movies from a Writer's POV." And I've updated some film, television, and book references.

I have also edited down the assignments, as some of them included requirements to comment on other students' work, attend a screening, or read something online that is no longer available. The assignments, then, are really suggestions for you on how to maintain your progress as a screenwriter if you're working alone. If you read this book one "lesson" at a time and do the assignments after each lesson, you will have a completed first draft of a screenplay when you finish the book.

If you do organize a writers group, you'll have input from others. Be sure to listen, but that doesn't mean you have to accept every suggestion. If one person makes an observation, that could be interesting if you feel it improves your work. If two people make the same observation, you might give it more thought. If three people make the same observation, it might be time to make a change.

Of course, you don't have to do it that way. You can just read the book straight through and then start a screenplay. It depends on your goals. Whichever way you choose, once you have completed a first draft, you probably will need to rewrite your screenplay. Everyone does, even the best in the business. If you do decide to rewrite your work, I suggest you pick up a copy of my book *Rewrite: A Step-by-Step Guide to Strengthen Structure, Characters, and Drama in Your Screenplay, 2nd Edition*, published by Michael Wiese Productions. You'll find some of what you read here in that book, as these lectures establish the basis of my method of approaching screenwriting. But there's a lot more in-depth discussion of what to do next in the process of writing a polished, ready-to-sell screenplay.

For the most part, I have left the lessons as they were except in cases where things in the industry or craft have changed so much as to leave certain parts inapplicable. Still, there remain some outdated references or comments appropriate to course-based or online learning. Please forgive those and move on to what's important—your work.

NOTE

From time to time a student would call me *sensei,* which is a Japanese word usually meaning teacher or master of a particular art or science. Directly translated, it means *the one who comes before*. I take it to mean the one who shines a light on the path. I've been down the path many times. I know it well. I know how to avoid the dead ends, the deviations that take you out of the way, the pitfalls and traps that prevent you from reaching your goal. That said, the path I'm shining the light on isn't the only path. My hope is that you find your own after traveling the one I show you.

ORIGINAL INTRODUCTION LETTER TO STUDENTS

I'm supposed to welcome you to this space, but I always get the nagging feeling that I should be warning you of the torture ahead. Oh yeah, this course is going to be torture, but that's only a hint of what's to come. Because the truth is, writing screenplays is a tough row to hoe. There's the coming up with the idea, beating it out, trying to pitch it, getting development executives' notes on which way to go with it, writing the damn thing, rewriting it, getting more notes that bring it down, getting notes that bring it up, rewriting it . . . It can be a nightmare. And that's when it all works and you're successful. When it doesn't work, when you don't sell something, you do all the work (though without all the bad notes), but you don't make any of the money.

So, I probably should say "Turn back!" But you're about to enter a rich and rewarding life, or hours and hours of agony. Or both. Screenwriters are notorious for hating to write but loving having written. The process tortures most of us, but we love the sense of fulfillment when we see (some of) our words up there on the screen. My advice to you is to continue only if you have a burning need to write and have something to say. If you're just doing it for the sex and the fast cars, go into acting.

In these courses we're going to work on creating a screenplay from scratch. We're going to start with premise, then work on characters, then the main plot points, then a beat sheet, then a treatment, then the pages of the script. We're going to do it exactly the way I approach an assignment from a production company or studio. It's going to be intense. And it's going to require some serious butt-in-the-seat time on a regular basis. I say this because it's very difficult to catch up once you've fallen behind more than a couple of weeks, and I want you to succeed in reaching your goal. That's why I ask you to develop early on the commitment to a schedule, the setting aside of five to ten hours a week on a regular basis, to write. Writers write. There's no way of getting around it. And besides, if you don't write, you can't enjoy having written.

So tell your significant other, your dog or cat, your children (the hardest, I know), your plants, etc., that you're going to need some alone time. You'll see them again in ten weeks (after each course).

You might want to know why I'm qualified to teach this, since you probably have never heard of me. Check out my website (PaulChitlik.com) for biographical and professional information. Or go to IMDb.com to see about half of my credits. (Some were written under a pseudonym, others didn't qualify at the time because of IMDb's rules about syndicated shows.)

I hope you have some ideas and a great imagination. In this course, we'll work on the craft that will enable you to put them to use.

Course 1

INTRODUCTION TO SCREENWRITING I

Lesson One

PREMISE—CHARACTER—CONFLICT

Welcome to the exciting and disturbing world of the screenwriter. In the novel, a writer works with words to create worlds in a reader's imagination, one reader at a time. In a screenplay, a writer works with words to create worlds in the minds of about one hundred and fifty to several thousand people, who then create a visible, audible world for millions. While the two achievements sound very similar, in several major senses they are not: The format in writing novels is free; in screenplays certain conventions apply. Structure in novels is open; in screenplays the three-act play dominates. In novels, what characters are thinking is one of the main storytelling tools; in screenplays, you only know your characters by what they say and do.

A good novel makes a reader think and feel. A good screenplay makes a reader think, feel, and *see,* one reader at a time as you work up the chain of people who are empowered to say "no" until you get to the person empowered to say "yes." Then it goes to the people who interpret your words and make them into visual and audio realities recorded on film or video and presented for the enjoyment and edification of your ultimate audience.

PREMISE

There's a very long road that stretches from the desire to write a film all the way to the Oscar. Having a map is a good idea. Knowing where you want to go with your film before you start to write it is essential. It's not only important to know the tone and genre—comedy, drama, horror, action, etc.—of the film, it's important to know what it's about. That's the premise. Some people call it the theme or central idea of the film.

Most people wouldn't go to the airport without knowing their destination. Sure, some people just like to see where fate brings them when they travel. Most, however, make plans. They know at least the destination, if not the side tours and hotels. All forms of disaster await the traveler who has no idea where they're heading, from unexpected expenses, to monumental wastes of time, to landing in the middle of an unfriendly and dangerous locale. It's good to know where you're going before you set out, just as it's good to know what your movie's about before you begin writing it. But, just as destinations can change and delightful surprises be found on your physical journeys, so can the premise of your movie evolve and new details emerge along the way.

If you truly don't know where you're going when you start writing, you haven't a chance in hell of getting there.

One way to know where you're going is to know what you want to say—know your theme, your premise. That's the compass. You might not want to reach the North Pole, but maybe you want to go in that general direction. That's what the premise will help you do.

If you do the assigned reading, you'll see how Lajos Egri, the Hungarian theater critic and author of *The Art of Dramatic Writing*, defines premise, plus several examples of premise in drama. While Egri deals strictly with play construction, I'm of the firm belief that his thoughts apply to films as well. (See my article on movie themes on page 9, part of the assignments for lesson 1). I'm not going to summarize Egri's text, except to give you a few examples of premise here for clarity: "Great love defies even death" for *Romeo and Juliet*. "Blind trust leads to destruction" for *King Lear*. "Ruthless ambition leads to its own destruction" for *Macbeth.* These short premises are what those plays are really about. Consciously or subconsciously, they guided Shakespeare in his writing. Each one would make a great movie (and have, repeatedly; you can bet on it). It's what the movie is really about.

Let's think of some films in this light. If we can't reduce a film to a one-line premise, then either we didn't understand it, or the film itself was muddled (a strong possibility).

Examples: "Underestimating nature leads to disaster" for *The Perfect Storm*. "Self-awareness leads to liberation" for *Barbie.* "Right conquers tyranny" for *The Patriot*. "Cooperation and hope will free you from bondage" for *Chicken Run*. (Yes, *Chicken Run*.) "Love conquers all, even death" for *Titanic* (and *Romeo and Juliet*). "You must accept who you are to achieve your dreams" for *CODA*. "You must struggle to find meaning in your work" for *Birdman.*

Think of a current film and see if you can reduce it to its premise.

The writer has a goal in each of the examples—to prove something. Isn't that one of the reasons *you* want to write? Sure, you want to entertain. Sure, you're in it for the money and glory. But don't you want to *say* something, too? And guess what? Unless you set out with something to say, you're going to end up with a boring film. It doesn't have to be deep, just some premise that can be proven. And you really have to believe it.

That makes it much easier to write a screenplay, having a beacon to guide you rather than stumbling around in the darkness. Sure, you can start a screenplay without knowing your premise, but if you don't find it along the way, it's not going to be very good. Every scene, every character, every attitude must point to it or they will seem out of place, unnecessary, irrelevant, distracting. Even in a movie that's just a character study. Even in a comedy. (Especially in a comedy.)

Take a second to look at the list of premises in *The Art of Dramatic Writing*. Choose one or bring your own to the table.

Once you've chosen your premise, you should believe in it. You're not going to be very convincing if you don't. And it must be an active premise, one that can be proven with action.

What if you just have a character, or maybe just a situation? What about the character attracts you? What do you think is interesting about that character? What goals does that character have, and what do they do to achieve them? What obstacles are in their way? The struggle that character goes through should define your premise. Do you see one forming in your mind now or not? If the answer is no, maybe you need to look at another character, even though the one you want to write about is very funny or quirky. Your Aunt Matilda or your friend Poindexter who's just *such* a character you know they'd make a great movie won't make a great movie unless there's a premise. If you can't think of a crucible to put that character into, an obstacle for them to overcome, and a reason to do so, look elsewhere.

If you're starting from a funny, romantic, scary, or haunting situation, ask yourself: Who is in this situation, how did they get there, and how are they going to get out of there? A premise can show you the way.

If you're going to write something based on a real-life story, so much the better. Something in the struggle of the story should point you in the right direction. Struggle to do what? If you don't have a struggle, even in a comedy, then you don't have a movie. Maybe an amusing anecdote, but not a movie.

PREMISE—CHARACTER—CONFLICT

The premise sets your character(s) in motion; your conflict defines them; their internal character determines the truth of your premise through their actions.

It's a lot to remember when you're starting out to write a screenplay, but the main thing to remember is: Have something to write about—a premise. Have people to write about—characters. Have your characters prove their mettle—conflict.

CHARACTER

As much as I've emphasized premise, I believe no movie ever makes it without interesting characters, and not just the main character. Sometimes it's the peripheral characters who are the most memorable, and that's something to keep in mind later when you're working on them. But, for now, let's look at our main character. And, yes, there has to be one. Sure, ensemble films are possible, but name two. Okay, *The Return of the Secaucus Seven* and *The Big Chill.* Name two more. Tough, isn't it? Look carefully at the Marvel Cinematic Universe movies. There's a team of characters, but there is usually one who is the central character. The one who is on a journey to learn more about themself. There has to be a central character. Now, who is it in your movie?

Pick one. You've been thinking about, say, "Right conquers tyranny." Or, to put it another way, "Right beats might." You need a character to prove that. You have to ask yourself: Why them? Why now for this person? What does this person want? How is the process of getting that going to change them?

The Mel Gibson character in *The Patriot,* created by screenwriter Robert Rodat (who also wrote, with some assists, *Saving Private Ryan*), is a complex and sympathetic character who, nevertheless, is capable of bloody excesses in battle that disgust even him. But let's ask the questions about this character.

- **Why him?** Because he was once on the other side. Because he's got a family to protect (i.e., the stakes are high for him), and because he knows about war.
- **Why now?** Because it is a time in history when sides must be taken. Because his son is killed by a ruthless British soldier. Because he has another son to rescue.
- **What does he want?** To rescue his boy. To avenge his other one. To provide safety and security for his family. Freedom.
- **How does the process change him?** He abandons his pacifist beliefs. His old bloodthirsty character reemerges. He loses all his

possessions. He loses another son. He gains a wife (though this is poorly brought out). He triumphs over tyranny.

Maybe you have the answers to these questions before you know who your character really is, maybe you have them after you write a character sketch, or maybe you won't know until the process is complete.

More on that next week. One step at a time. Right now, it's the thinking stage—about what and about whom am I going to write?

Assignment

1. Read the first chapter of *The Art of Dramatic Writing* by Lajos Egri, where he introduces the concept of premise.
2. Read the first ten pages or watch the first ten minutes of *Tin Cup* (https://www.dailyscript.com/scripts/Tin_Cup.pdf) and *His Girl Friday* (https://www.dailyscript.com/scripts/His%20Girl%20Friday.txt).
3. Read "A Paucity of Premises," which originally appeared in the *Los Angeles Times* in 1998 (see page 9).
4. Write the premise of your film.
5. If you've formed a writers group, share your premise with the group. Are they meaningful? Are they active? Try not to use any form of the verb "to be" (is, are, was, were, has been, will be).

A Paucity of Premises

By Paul Chitlik

Maybe David Fieber's problem with the movies ("Is 'Armageddon' Really the End?," Counterpunch, July 13) isn't that they are shot and edited MTV-style, poorly directed, acted, or even written. Maybe the problem is that they are all about the same thing. I noticed several years ago that sitcom episodes have only two themes: "Ya gotta be yourself" and "Everything is OK as long as we're together in the end." Go ahead, point out the exceptions. Memorable, aren't they?

There are reasons for this: The grinding machine that is sitcom production doesn't allow much time for the exploration of real themes, the networks are uncomfortable with anything that requires true thought on the part of the viewer, and jokes are hard to come by when you're talking about the nature of being.

So, it's just easier to stick to what works, over and over again. I always thought films wouldn't get caught in this trap. I was wrong, especially this summer. I mean, humans face dilemmas other than the struggle to be themselves, don't they?

I thought *The Truman Show*, written by Andrew Niccol, was on to something, that it had the potential to be a really great movie. But the most interesting aspect of the film went completely unexplored: How did the actors surrounding Truman deal with their double lives? How did they deal with deceiving the one they were paid to love? Instead, it's a film about, yes, say it because it's true, "Ya gotta be yourself."

What is *Dr. Dolittle* (the 1998 version), written by Larry Levin and Nat Mauldin, about? Is it about the nature of man and his relationship with animals? Is it about the rights of animals to exist on a planet of species-centered humans, or is it about Dr. Dolittle recognizing and accepting who he really is? If you guessed "C," you're ready to be a studio executive.

Mulan, written by Rita Hsiao, Chris Sanders, Philip LaZebnik, and the writing team of Raymond Singer & Eugenia Bostwick-Singer, with a story by Robert D. San Souci, was a groundbreaking movie for Disney, but its theme, well, what could be more plain? We all cringed when she was taken to the matchmaker who tried to turn the young woman into her culture's vision of what a beautiful, submissive wife should be. Obviously not Mulan. Then she disguised herself as a man to fight in her father's place, but it wasn't until she was revealed as a woman that she truly came into her own. She had to be herself. Listen to the theme song.

There are exceptions. You can point them out; I can point them out. But look at *Godzilla* (the 1998 one). If we accept that the main character is the Matthew Broderick character, we have no theme. If it's Godzilla, then it's back to "Ya gotta be yourself." Maybe that's why its box office didn't approach expectations. The film wasn't about anything other than special effects.

On the other hand, isn't that what *Titanic*, written by James Cameron, would have been without its love-conquers-all theme? That's what attracted audiences around the world, though it does have a lingering "It's OK because we're together in the end" motif.

Why the paucity of theme? Could it be the emphasis on style over content, effects over story, producers and directors over writers?

It's hard to keep track of complex themes if a writer is called in just to work on the dialogue of a specific character. The writer will just be servicing that character, rather than the theme or story suggested by the original writer.

Or maybe it is the writer who is at fault, even if there are nine of them on a film. Instead of relying on the old standbys, why not write about love conquers all, good triumphs over evil, guilt and expiation, avarice destroys the soul, poverty stinks, thought separates us from the animals, there is no such thing as good and evil, liars lie to themselves, the human spirit can triumph over adversity, humanity transcends race, rust never sleeps, a bird in the hand—whatever, just so long as it isn't "Ya gotta be yourself."

If you're worried that would make for boring drama, look at Shakespeare, Shaw, Preston Sturges, Herman Mankiewicz, Robert Towne, Nora Ephron, Frank Darabont, Woody Allen, Chloé Zhao, David Koepp, Jane Goldman—choose your favorite screenwriter.

Just don't look at today's blockbusters.

Lesson Two

MATCHING THE CHARACTER TO THE PREMISE

Now you know the idea behind your film, but, really, isn't it more important to know *who* it's about rather than *what* it's about? Actually, the two go hand in hand. You must match your premise to your central character (or the other way around). Once you have an idea of what your movie is about, you must find the characters who will help you prove your premise. I'm not saying you can't go the other way around—find your characters and then your premise. It's just harder to do it that way. I've done it and so have lots of other people. But if you know what your characters have to achieve ahead of time, it makes it easier to find the kind of characters you need.

For example: *Romeo and Juliet*. If Romeo had been thoughtful and cautious (say, like Hamlet), the story would have gone nowhere. The premise of "Great love defies even death" would never have been proven with Hamlet as the central character. If George Clooney's character had been cautious, there would have been no story in *The Perfect Storm*.

The personalities of these characters drive these stories. Their actions prove the premises. And only these characters work.

Maybe you're thinking that these characters created these plots, and you would be right. Certainly, without the Clooney character, there is no plot, just a big storm. Without the Mel Gibson character's background, without his love for his family, without his slip into a killing frenzy, there would be no *The Patriot*.

But how do you know if the character you're creating is right for your story? You have to explore that character. Get to know them as best you can. That's why it's important to have a *character sketch* of your main characters before you start writing. They'll change as you write, but you need guidelines.

Here's what to put in your character sketch:

- The time in which your character exists (era, century, decade, contemporary).
- Age, gender, general physical characteristics.
- Some of the events that shaped the character.
- Some relationships that speak to the character.
- Some achievements or occupation; recreational likes and dislikes; preferred food.
- Emotional life of the character—quick to anger, slow to anger, weepy over soap operas, closed down emotionally.

Egri breaks it down into three main areas: physiology, sociology, and psychology. In other words, what does you character look like, what are the circumstances they have lived through and now find themselves in, and what is their personality and reasons for that personality? See the reading assignment for more details on this. It's important.

Be sure to give your character room to grow, because that's what's going to be the process of your film—how the character grows. Give your heroes flaws and your villains love in their hearts for someone, something. What do they like to wear, eat, watch on TV? Why should we like them? Why should we hate them?

One thing to remember. Most moviegoers (me in particular) don't like movies about jerks. We want characters we like, characters we can relate to, or, at least, characters who are extremely interesting.

Characters who are sympathetic. If we don't like the main character, what's the point of watching the movie? Always ask yourself as you create the character, and the film itself, is this a person or film I'd go to see myself? If not, drop it and think of another, because you're going to be living with that character for many months, even years. Also, if you don't care about them, who would?

Premise and character. You practically have a movie already if you know what these two things are.

"Character is the fundamental material we are forced to work with, so we must know character as thoroughly as possible." —Lajos Egri, *The Art of Dramatic Writing.*

Movies are not abstractions like twentieth century art. They are based on people—their interactions, their responses to conflict. Their emotions. The building blocks of movies are characters. Interesting, vital, dynamic, funny, weird, scary, stupid, bizarre characters.

It's not enough to know your character's traits, you must (and the audience must, sometimes) know why they have those traits. Actors often write character bios to understand their character. They need to get inside the character in order to *be* that character. So do you. How else will you be able to think, talk, and act like that character? How else will you be able to write an authentic, interesting person?

We have to know where the character is coming from to know where they're going to. Their reactions have to make sense and have consistency. You base that on what you've created about the character's background (physical, situational, and psychological).

"If we wish to understand the actions of any individual, we must look at the motivation which compels him to act as he does." —Egri.

The easiest way to do this is to choose a character from your life and write about them. Egri has detailed descriptions (pages 52–57 in the 1960 English version of *The Art of Dramatic Writing*), but you can just look at the sketches at the end of this chapter. You needn't write all the details, but you should know your characters as well as you know your best friend. That way all your character's actions will make sense and be logical, given their background.

And the character must change over the course of your story. This process of change is commonly referred to as the "character arc." Just as real people change in response to their environment and the challenges they face, your characters should change and grow in the crucible of your movie.

How do we know this is happening? Because a character grows and is revealed through action and conflict. How your character struggles, what they do to overcome the odds, that's what tells us about them. If they're strong (and they must be) then they put up a decent fight, an interesting fight, a fight worthy of your audience's attention for ninety minutes.

The conflict can come from within or without. It doesn't matter. The character can make mistakes in their responses to crises. So much the better. So long as they respond. "A weak character is one who, for any reason, cannot make a decision to act," Egri writes. And why would we want to watch someone who does nothing in the face of adversity? They've got to at least try to do something.

"Did you catch your character at that particular moment when he was ready for conflict?" —Egri, again.

Let's assume, now, that you know who your characters are, what their backgrounds are, their personalities, and their current situations. Now you have to introduce them in such a way that we can know their essence in just a few bits of action, just a few words of dialogue, so we can set our stories in motion.

Let's look at the first ten pages of *His Girl Friday*, screenplay by Charles Lederer from the play *The Front Page* by Ben Hecht & Charles MacArthur. If you're reading it digitally, there are no page numbers, so read for about five minutes. If you're reading it in the *Scenario* magazine format, we're talking about the first ten columns or so. (In a normal screenplay format, the rule of thumb—often wildly inaccurate—is that one page equals one minute of screen time. In a Howard Hawks film, though, they talk way too fast for that to apply.) If you're viewing the video, we're talking about the opening of the film until Burns leads Hildy out of the city room.

In the screenplay, MacArthur gets us into the world immediately, and in the first page we hear the cynicism of an anonymous reporter. Seconds later, we meet Hildy Johnson, whose first line of dialogue tells us she used to work there. She also tells us something about Burns immediately: "Tell me, is the lord of the universe in today?" Those few words expose her opinion of him. Soon, we have a good idea about Bruce, too, partly through dialogue and partly through actions like opening the gate to the city room. As we follow Hildy through the city room, we see she was a popular employee; then we find she's divorced and about to see her ex-husband, the "lord of the universe." Intriguing, isn't it?

Then we're introduced to Burns, about whom we already know quite a bit. Now we see it confirmed: The "lord of the universe" has a lackey helping him shave.

If you've answered the question "why them?" for your own character, you're ready to ask "why now?" Why do we pick up these characters at this moment in time?

For Burns we immediately find out the "why now" question—there's a crisis over a scheduled hanging. For Hildy, the "why now" is she's about to get married, and she wants Burns to stop harassing her. In seconds we know what these two people want and what the conflict of the film is: He wants her back; she wants to get away from his influence. Or so she thinks.

We quickly see, too, the character of Bruce Baldwin in contrast with Burns. A detail as simple as the action of holding, or not holding, the swinging door out of the newsroom says loads about who these men are.

So, Hildy's and Burns's goals are opposed. And Bruce's and Burns's goals are opposed. The central conflict is established.

In *Tin Cup*, written by John Norville and Ron Shelton, the screenplay starts with Tin Cup (his nickname) driving balls and drinking beer. His attitude toward golf is delineated sharply. Romeo's character is set up in his first line and his handful of cash. And Molly is set up with one line—"The doctor's a woman," which also sets her in conflict with Tin Cup. We see her as the complete opposite (and the doctor *is* a woman, in her case) in golf, too—she's got all new paraphernalia. Her appearance tells her story. Then their opening exchange sets them on opposite sides of the feminist question, and they're off!

As Tin Cup describes how to drive a ball, he tells us about himself in the process, right down to saying he never finishes anything, an important part of his personality, the part that looks like it might be in for a change.

In their first exchange, he teaches her how to let go; she questions his whole existence.

What does he want? Cash. That's it. He thinks. It could change, but that's all he seems to want right now. What does she want? To learn to play golf. But we've also learned that he has a reputation. That he could and should be richer, and that she can verbally fence with the best.

Now, let's look a little more closely at the main characters from our two films. Are they likeable? And what defines their likeability?

Hildy is likeable right away. She's friendly, sharp, vulnerable. Others like her, so we do. Burns is more problematical. Though he lets loose a smile to show us how he feels about Hildy, he's still pretty gruff. But the smile hints at what's really inside—a man vulnerable, in love, and desperate to get his wife back. (And we hear how desperate he is—hiring a skywriter to try to influence the divorce court judge!) And we know that Hildy likes him, so there has to be something good in there. He's both likeable and interesting. (And handsome, as played by Cary Grant.)

Tin Cup isn't so immediately likeable. He seems mercenary at first, with the hangers-on at the driving range. Then he seems to put Molly down. It isn't until he introduces a little humor—calling "shit" and "fuck" highly technical golf terms—that we begin to see him in a positive light. And we're really sold when he recites his ode to the golf swing. This is no ordinary driving range hack, this is a poet and an artist. That makes for an interesting combination. One to whom we'd like to see what happens.

Molly is no less interesting—a psychologist with her own set of problems. Not necessarily a novel idea, but at least she's self-aware.

She's sharp-tongued and comfortable with who she is. She's going to give Tin Cup a run for his money. And we'd like to see that run.

We see that in this story, it's mostly going to be the two of them, though Romeo plays an important part, as does Molly's fiancé, and Tin Cup's rival, David Simms. In *His Girl Friday*, there's a cast of characters who help along the story.

So, let's assume you know who your characters are. How is your audience going to know? By the actions of your characters. What they do, what they say, how they change—this is what tells moviegoers about the people they've invested fifteen dollars (fifteen, I tell you!) to get to know.

The worlds the people from *Tin Cup* and *His Girl Friday* live in are quite clear by the time we're five minutes into each film. How are you going to show us who your people are?

Before you show us who these people are, though, you have to create them. You generally do that by writing a character sketch or biography of the character. Lajos Egri, in *The Art of Dramatic Writing*, says there are three components to every character—the physiological, the sociological, and the psychological. In other words, what they look like physically—height, sometimes weight, race, age, etc.; where they come from and what their circumstances are now—where they were born, what kind of family they come from, what kind of education they have had, their occupation, where they live now; and what their thought processes and emotions are—whether they're a happy person, depressed, manic, psychotic, intelligent, slow, warm, introverted. It's also good to include their goals and the flaws or quirks that set them apart.

Since this is something that you never, *ever* show to producers, it can be as brief or as detailed as you want, but it must contain the three main elements: physiology, sociology, and psychology. See pages 20–22 for examples.

Assignment

1. Read the first half of the second chapter of *The Art of Dramatic Writing* by Lajos Egri, up to part 6, "Plot or Character."
2. Write character sketches of your main characters: the protagonist, the antagonist, and the central emotional relationship person (the person with whom your protagonist has to create or mend a relationship, sometimes called the love interest, but they could be a friend, a brother, a parent, etc.).
3. Watch *Risky Business.*
4. If you've started a writers group, read each other's sketches. Are the protagonists interesting people? Is the antagonist worthy enough of a challenge? Is the central emotional relationship character important enough?

Character Sketch of Benjamin Martin from *The Patriot*

screenplay by Robert Rodat

THE GHOST, BENJAMIN MARTIN

Physiology: 40s. Dark hair. Rugged looking. In good shape.

Sociology: Plantation owner but does not own slaves. Widower. Father of 6. Former army captain. Legislator. Famous.

Psychology: Suffers from posttraumatic stress as a result of the French and Indian War. Afraid that sins will revisit him (and they do). Slow to anger, but a mighty temper. Failed furniture maker but doesn't give up. Sentimental. Soft-spoken. Pacifist until forced. *Family, freedom, and frenzy* would be an accurate short list of his concerns.

Flaw that He Must Overcome: His blood lust.

Goal: To stay out of war → to rescue son → to win war.

Character Sketch of George Bailey from *It's a Wonderful Life*

Screenplay by Frances Goodrich, Albert Hackett, and Frank Capra. Additional scenes by Jo Swerling. Based on a story by Philip Van Doren Stern.

GEORGE BAILEY

Physiology: Starts as a child. Loses hearing (after saving brother). Grows tall and slender.

Sociology: Middle class, intact family. Father is the head of a savings and loan (George goes to work in his office). Has a maid. Has a younger brother, whom he saves. Works in a drugstore as a child, takes over father's business. People like him (Mary whispers into his ear; Violet likes him, too). Lives in a small town. Never gets to attend college or to travel.

Psychology: Interested in travel, adventure. Willing to risk life to save others. Compassionate. Speaks his mind. Happy and not afraid to show it. Loves his father. Loyal. Sincere. Patriotic.

Flaw: Has a temper.

Goal: To do something big and important.

Character Sketch of Remy from *Ratatouille*

Written and Directed by Brad Bird, Story by Jan Pinkava and Jim Capobianco & Brad Bird

REMY

Physiology: He appears to be a little smaller than the other rats, especially his brother. He could be an adolescent, we're not sure, but he is certainly a rat. He stands out because he can walk on his hind legs like a human. He does this so his hands are free.

Sociology: He belongs to an extended rat family. His mother is never mentioned, but his father is prominent, as is his brother, who eventually leads him into trouble. He lives with the family in the attic of a farmhouse but spends most of his time on a trash pile with the others eating. His father is the leader of the whole extended family of rats. He's never lived anywhere else.

Psychology: He has discovered the miracle of combining flavors and exalts in it. He has a highly sensitive nose, which his father uses as a test for poison in their food, but which he prefers to use to smell ingredients and then in tasting the food that he prepares from them. He is enthralled by Chef Gusteau and wants to be a cook.

Flaw: Willing to steal, if necessary, in order to achieve his goals.

Goal: To become a chef.

A classic Pixar film, *Ratatouille* features a rat in the central role. One of the great accomplishments of the film, and there are many, is that it makes a rat, Remy, a sympathetic character with a minimum of exposition.

Lesson Three

STORY

Now you have a premise, characters, and goals. That's almost everything needed to create a story. What is a story? Here's a definition I and many others have used: There's a person. They have a goal (i.e., they want something). There's a rock (a barrier) between them and their goal. They have to go over, under, around, or through the rock to get to the goal.

That process of going over, under, around, or through—that's the story.

STRUCTURE

Obviously, the goal of a romantic comedy is to unite the two protagonists by the end of the film. So, in a sense, romantic comedies are the easiest to plot out—we just constantly throw obstacles in between our characters. But that gets tired fast unless the characters have other goals. In *His Girl Friday*, Burns wants to obtain clemency for, and a story about, a condemned man. A noble goal, though not necessarily pursued by the most noble of means. Tin Cup decides to win the U.S. Open and has to go through hell and fight his own demons to do it. And both must woo their women.

We've met the characters. We know the goals. Now something has got to set the stories in motion. Sometimes this is called the inciting incident, the occurrence or challenge that forces the characters to make a change in their life, to stop the ordinary and strive for something different. It could be as simple as a traffic jam that ticks off D-FENS as in *Falling Down*, screenplay by Ebbe Roe Smith. It could be a series of unusual events followed by a visit with Weird Barbie, as in Greta Gerwig and Noah Baumbach's *Barbie.* It could be the crash landing of a space craft (*Independence Day*, screenplay by Roland Emmerich & Dean Devlin). It's often getting fired from a job (*American Beauty*, screenplay by Alan Ball). Something's got to put the story in motion as soon as we know our characters. Sooner, if we can learn about our characters as we go.

STRUCTURE (AGAIN)

Did I say structure was important? Just in case I didn't, let me say it now. If I have, let me say it again. Structure is important.

We've all heard the dreaded word, but, in fact, structure simplifies screenwriting. Just as an architect knows certain structural forms will serve as the basis for certain types of edifices, so, too, screenwriters know that the simple three-act play structure works best for films.

Try to build a skyscraper or a bridge without a plan, without relying on the steel skeletons that have proven through the years to be the best. Try doing it from the top down, or try starting willy-nilly in the middle. Ain't gonna work. Can't work. Relying on formulaic structure doesn't restrict the writer, it frees them to work within a form that they know will work. The Chrysler Building doesn't look like the One World Trade Center, but the basic structures rely on the same formulas. The Brooklyn Bridge and the Golden Gate—both built to strict rules of bridge building, but very different in appearance.

The form we most use in screenwriting has been adapted from playwriting, and, as such, has been in development for 2,500 years. It works. You can possibly do a screenplay utilizing another format, but why waste time trying to perfect it? Why not focus on creating novel characters, interesting situations, unpredictable twists and turns? This is the Hollywood standard. Some other cultures have different formats, but the Hollywood paradigm is followed throughout most of the world.

So here's how it goes in its simplest form. There are three acts to a typical screenplay. Each act has a beginning, a middle, and an end. Each starts with the character trying to achieve a goal, going through the process of reaching that goal, and either reaching it (and realizing that more is yet to be done) or not reaching it and setting out to reach it again.

Act I sets up both your characters in their ordinary life and the conflict, which is introduced by the inciting incident. By the end of the act, the action has swollen to a crisis that sets up the sharp confrontation in act II. Your character has a goal and a plan.

Act II plays out the conflict. Your protagonist attempts to reach their goal but meets obstacle after obstacle. In the middle of act II, commonly called the turning point, the action should flip, take an unpredictable but logical turn that puts everything into jeopardy, changes everything, heads the action off into a new and interesting direction. The end of act II finds your hero at their lowest point, where it looks like they'll never be able to reach their goal. And quite possibly their life is in danger, too.

Act III begins with something that reawakens your character's determination and is jammed with actions that try to resolve the conflict and lead to an inevitable and satisfying final challenge and climax. Then there's a return to normal life, though "normal" may be redefined by now. In fact, it's now changed forever.

The act curtain—the closing of each act—leaves you in suspense: Now what? And we should have that at the ends of acts I and II. At the end of act III, we should have a good idea what will happen with the rest of this person's life.

Do we really need to do it this way? No. You can find your own way. But while you flounder around for the next fifty years trying to invent a new genre, others will be fulfilling their dreams writing screenplays that follow this single format.

Let's look at the movie I asked you to view before this lesson and see how it adheres to the framework we've been discussing.

In *Risky Business*, written by Paul Brickman, we're introduced to Joel Goodsen, played by Tom Cruise. His immediate concerns are clearly set out in the first sequence: a lengthy dream he narrates for his poker-playing buddies. He dreams about having sex with a woman and about missing out on going to college because of a single mistake. Fear controls him—fear of sex and fear of failure to get into an Ivy League school. He takes the safe path, always, out of fear.

There are at least two possible instances of an inciting incident. One could be solely dialogue, when Miles tells Joel that every once in a while you have to take a chance on things, say "what the fuck" and just do it. A later act by Miles really gets the action going; he uses Joel's name when he calls a prostitute whose number he's gotten from the newspaper. Eventually this leads to the climax (in more ways than one) of the first act when Joel and Lana, played by Rebecca De Mornay, prove that Joel had nothing to fear from sex. One goal is achieved. The first act ends when Joel returns from the bank to find something missing—a crystal egg that his mother prizes highly.

Now Joel has a new goal—he has to retrieve the egg. This is the beginning of the second act. We reach the midpoint when Lana proposes that they work out a way to get their friends together for fun and profit. He's forced into it when his father's car falls into Lake Michigan. The action spins off into a completely different direction.

The end of the second act is another dual climax. Assured that he won't be admitted to Princeton by a rep from the college who has visited during a party Joel has thrown, Joel has accepted and even embraced his future at the University of Illinois. Regarding one of his goals, all is lost, but he's okay with it. On the train to Chicago, he and Lana couple again. But on his return home, he finds that everything has been stolen from his parents' home.

End of act II. Now he's got another goal—to get it all back before his parents return. He confronts Guido and buys back everything. But he's not a scared kid here, he's an adult, dealing one-on-one with another adult. So he succeeds, though not completely: The egg is cracked. Things look bleak, but he then finds out that the Princeton rep has called and told his father that "Princeton needs guys like him." He's in. Both goals achieved, he's gone from being a fearful boy to a self-assured man, and we've all enjoyed the journey.

Is this the only way to write a screenplay? No. This is the format most used in Hollywood, but it is by no means the only format. *The Hero's Journey* has received lots of press since Joseph Campbell first put forward the idea that mythological stories in almost any culture follow the same basic format. His ideas were refined and applied specifically to screenplays by Christopher Vogler in *The Writer's Journey*. One of the best examples of this in a film occurs in *Star Wars* (the original).

The twelve-step format goes roughly like this:

ACT I

1. Heroes are introduced in **The Ordinary World**, where . . .
2. They receive **The Call to Adventure**.
3. They are **Reluctant** at first or **Refuse the Call**, but . . .
4. Are encouraged by a **Mentor** to . . .
5. Cross the first threshold and enter the **Special World**, where . . .

ACT II

6. They encounter **Tests, Allies, and Enemies**.
7. They **Approach the Inmost Cave**, crossing the second threshold . . .
8. Where they endure **The Supreme Ordeal** (metaphorical death and rebirth).
9. They take possession of their **Reward** (seizing the sword) and . . .
10. Are pursued on **The Road Back** to the Ordinary World.

ACT III

11. They cross the third threshold, experience a **Resurrection**, and are transformed by the experience (second life-and-death moment—this mirrors the supreme ordeal).

12. They **Return with the Elixir**, a boon or treasure to benefit the Ordinary World.

There may be other paradigms, or you might be the one to discover a new one, but I recommend, for simplicity's sake, that you concentrate on the three-act structure and focus your creative energies on creating interesting situations and unique characters.

So, again, the simplest form is the three-act structure, which further breaks down into seven points:

ACT I

1. Normal life introduces your character.
2. An inciting incident changes your character's life forever and compels them to take action.
3. Something forces the character to decide on a goal and devise a plan to reach it.

ACT II

1. One barrier after another prevents them from reaching their goal.
2. At the midpoint, something happens that makes the action spin off in a new direction. The goal changes from something the character wants to something the character needs.
3. The end of the act finds your character at their lowest point—all is lost. It looks like they will never reach their goal.

ACT III

1. The character rebounds from the depths with renewed energy to fight the last battle.
2. In the final challenge and climax, your character defeats the antagonist and reaches their goal.
3. They return to their normal, now changed forever, life.

See pages 30–31 for examples using actual films.

Assignment

1. Read the second half of the second chapter of *The Art of Dramatic Writing* by Lajos Egri, starting with part 6, "Plot or Character."
2. Write the main plot points (the seven points)—everyday life, inciting incident, act I curtain (goal and plan), midpoint or turning point, act II curtain (low point), final challenge, and return to normal life (now changed forever)—in one line each. Okay, maybe two lines.
3. Share your plot points with the writers group if you have one. In your discussions, be positive and honest with your critiques. Helping each other get to the best story possible is the goal here.

THE SEVEN POINTS OF *THELMA & LOUISE*

WRITTEN BY CALLIE KHOURI

1. **Ordinary Life:** Thelma starts off as the repressed housewife to car salesman and district manager Darryl, a male chauvinist pig if there ever was one. She even has to ask his permission to go away for the weekend with her friend, Louise, a waitress with an attitude and a steady boyfriend.
2. **Inciting Incident:** When a stranger takes Thelma outside a country bar to get some air, he tries to rape her, but Louise stops it by putting a bullet through the man's heart.
3. **End of Act I:** Thelma agrees to go to Mexico after she tells Darryl to "go fuck yourself."
4. **Midpoint or Turning Point:** Thelma has a sexual awakening with J.D., but he also steals their cash. Thelma takes charge, and they go on a crime spree.
5. **Low Point:** Thelma learns that the police know they're going to Mexico. They're doomed.
6. **Final Challenge:** Thelma suggests that they don't give up and get caught, that they should "keep goin'." She and Louise kiss, hold hands, and drive into the canyon.
7. **Return to the (Now Changed Forever) Normal Life:** Thelma and Louise are dead, but they are free of men for the first time. The implication is that the audience is now changed forever because of their journey.

The Seven Points of *CODA*

WRITTEN BY SIÂN HEDER, BASED ON THE BELGIUM FILM *LA FAMILLE BÉLIER*, WRITTEN BY VICTORIA BEDOS, THOMAS BIDEGAIN, STANISLAS CARRÉ DE MALBERG, AND ÉRIC LARTIGAU

1. **Ordinary Life:** Ruby is introduced singing on the family boat. We soon see her flaw—she feels inadequate.
2. **Inciting Incident:** Family business presents problem—inspectors are going to be on boats. In the personal story, Mr. V asks Ruby if she has something to say.

2a. **Inciting Incident for Central Emotional Relationship:** Mr. V pairs Ruby with Miles. (This comes late—twenty-five minutes in.)

3. **End of Act I:** Family business story, goal and plan—to sell fish directly
4. **Midpoint:** Family business—they have new plan to sell fish themselves with co-op.
5. **Low Point:** Family business—their license is stripped. They need a hearing person on board.
6. **Final Challenge:** At Ruby's final audition, she overcomes personal problems and signs her audition song.
7. **Return to the (Now Changed Forever) Normal Life:** CER—Ruby spends time with boyfriend at quarry. She spends time with parents before leaving for school.

Lesson Four

ARE YOUR CHARACTERS CHARACTERS?

Just in case you haven't burned the following in twelve-inch letters on the wall in front of your computer, I'll remind you of Egri's words: "Character is the fundamental material we are forced to work with, so we must know character as thoroughly as possible."

Another thing we must remember as we craft, shape, mold, and create the people who will populate our movies: They must be right for the premise. Egri's examples of characters in the correct contexts are good. What kind of dull play would *Romeo and Juliet* have been if Romeo had been a thinker like Hamlet? What would *Hamlet* have been with Romeo in the lead? To bring it up to date, what if the central character in *Memento*, Leonard, could actually remember what happened to him? Different movie altogether. What if Barbie already knew who she was? Or lacked confidence?

The personalities of these characters drive these stories. Their actions prove the premises. And only these characters work. People watch movies to see what happens to people they care about.

Who is the central character in your story? Why do we care about this person? Why are we eager to know how his conflict is resolved? What is it about this character that we like or admire? Or find interesting? And do we really have to like this character? Think about it. How many films are successful that have unredeemed assholes as their central character (other than *Scarface*)? They might start out as assholes, but they usually end up as something else. And even when they start out as assholes, like the Jim Carrey character in *Liar Liar*, there's something we like about them—their sense of humor, their looks, their vulnerability. And, importantly, their flaws and quirks. Flaws make a character more interesting. Even the good guy has some bad qualities. Part of their conflict is fighting those qualities.

If it's the antagonist we're talking about—the villain—then a whole flip side of questions must be asked. Why do we hate this character? Why do we want this character to lose? Why do they stir some emotion in us? And what's this character like when they are at home with their family? What's their good side? Because even the bad guy has some good qualities.

Why do these people engage in this conflict? Because they must, when faced with the circumstances. They must because of where they come from and who they are. They must because of what they want. So we must also know what a character wants and why.

"If we wish to understand the actions of any individual, we must look at the motivation which compels him to act as he does." —Egri.

The person on screen (or in a play, as described by Egri) is an amalgam of three different sets of characteristics: physiology, sociology, and psychology. In other words, what they look like physically, where they come from and their circumstances now, and what their thought processes are. For example, let's look again at the Mel Gibson character in *The Patriot* (screenplay by Robert Rodat). And look for a memorable quirk—something really different.

1. **Physiology:** Good-looking, early 40s, healthy.
2. **Sociology:** A man of property, a state representative, a father, a farmer, a veteran.
3. **Psychology:** A peaceful man, but he keeps a bloodthirst buried deep within.

4. **What He Wants:** Peace. Wants to protect his family. Wants to survive.

How did the screenwriter show us these traits? What actions or dialogue tell us of each of these? Why do these traits motivate him to act as he does?

Now, do the characters you've created fit the movie you have in mind? Not only do they have to serve your premise, but they must also serve your plot and genre. It seems obvious that Dorothy is the perfect protagonist of *The Wizard of Oz*. She could never have been the center of *Gone with the Wind*. The words "Lions and tigers and bears, oh my" wouldn't have come easily to Scarlett O'Hara, either. Julia Roberts as the Pretty Woman was great, but could the character she played in that film have tackled PG&E as Erin Brockovich did?

It all sounds so obvious, doesn't it? But it really is harder than hell to make sure your characters belong in the world you create for them. By *belong* I mean that, though your characters may sometimes be unpredictable (and they should be), everything they do or say makes sense within the world you've set up. Are they old enough or young enough to make your story work? Are they sweet enough or mean enough to appeal as a hero or a villain? Do they have a quirk that lets us get inside them, some characteristic we can grasp easily to show us their humanity? A flaw they overcome to prove how great they are?

Speaking of Erin Brockovich (and let's pretend for a moment I'm speaking here), what are the two things we most remember about her? . . . Okay, besides those two. And that's because of the first notable thing: the way she is dressed. She is making a statement and manipulating the other character in the scene by distracting him with her body. Clearly set up by Susannah Grant, with an assist by Richard LaGravenese (and based on the real person), Erin is flamboyant and not at all afraid to show her body. And the other most notable trait follows suit: She uses flamboyant language as well, and she's not afraid to speak her mind. A character to remember. So, why do we like the film? Not because of a boring legal proceeding, but because of a sympathetic character we can root for.

IN THE BEGINNING

Movies are about change. If we wanted stasis, we'd stay at home and watch television. Or the faucet drip. The protagonist of your film is at a point in their life when they need to make a change, or someone forces a change on them.

So, in the beginning, our character must make a choice or have a choice thrust upon them. They must want something, and the choice to go after it is going to propel the movie. Think of the Cary Grant character in *North by Northwest* (screenplay by Ernest Lehman). He is plucked out of his cushy life in a case of mistaken identity, and, before he knows what hit him, he's dodging a crop duster. He just wants to get back to his life. That's the beginning.

The middle is all the running and arguing and hiding out and outsmarting.

The end is the face of Mount Rushmore.

The skeleton of the movie isn't overly complex. The meat and bones, though, are great.

Grant's character wants something. He sets out to achieve that something. There are roadblocks in his way. He overcomes those roadblocks. There's a setback. He struggles anew. He succeeds, or he fails but finds he's achieved something altogether different, better, in the process. That's a movie in a nutshell. Think in those terms about the last film you saw.

THE ARC DE CHARACTER

If you've spent any time at all in Hollywood—virtual or real—you've heard the term "character arc." You already know what it means if you've read this far. It's what effect the trials and tribulation of the story have on the *character* of the character. In other words, how does what happens affect our protagonist? How do they change from a pompous, self-centered cynic as, say, the Bill Murray character in Danny Rubin's

Groundhog Day (rewrite by Harold Ramis) does to the caring, loving man at the end, capable of true despair and, ultimately, true happiness? There's the arc—from A to Z, but with lots of stops along the way. By the way, watch *Groundhog Day* for a look at a truly unique way to study a character.

LET'S MAKE THE SCENE

A movie is composed of scenes and groups of scenes called sequences, each of which has its own structure, its own beginning, middle, and end. Have I mentioned the word *conflict*? Not for quite a while. There's another word you should print out in 36-point bold and put in front of you when you write, because there is no scene without conflict, there is no story, there is no character arc, there is no movie, there is no Oscar at the end of the rainbow.

Just as there are barriers (conflict) for the protagonist to overcome over the length of the film, so, too, there are smaller conflicts in each scene. In the beginning of a scene, somebody wants something. Somebody else either tries to prevent them from getting that or wants something in opposition. The scene, then, is about the struggle. Learning what each one (or more) wants is the beginning of the scene. The struggle to get it is the middle. One or the other character wins the struggle. That's the end of the scene. Somebody's got to win, somebody's got to lose. Even in a comedy.

There is only one kind of scene you need for your movie—a scene that moves the plot forward. I don't care if you've got a great scene that is really funny, or dramatic, or tear-jerking. If it doesn't move the story along its way, we don't need it. If we don't need it, we don't put it in. No matter how brilliant they are, only necessary scenes are allowed: no side trips to grandma's house, no stopping to smell the flowers along the way, no trips to the comedy store or theme park—unless they are essential for the story. Bad scenes that move the story forward can be fixed. Great scenes that don't move the story are irreparable. They slow down the movie (or the reader of your script) and tend to make an audience fidget or wonder "What the hell?" Stick to your story. "When in doubt, leave it out," my boss used to tell me at my first writing job (as a news service reporter). Good advice for just about every situation.

Did I say there was only one kind of scene needed for a movie? I was wrong. There are two kinds of scenes. Of course, one kind moves the story. The other kind tells us something new about a character, usually the protagonist. If it doesn't move the story or tell us something we need to know about the character, we don't need the scene.

So, how many scenes do you need to write for a typical ninety-to-one-hundred-minute screenplay? Generally, more than one and fewer than one hundred. Joel Schumacher shot a film that takes place in a phone booth for ninety minutes. (And yes, it's called *Phone Booth.*) It turns out to be one well-constructed scene that reflects the typical structure of a well-made film. For contrast, look at *The Fall Guy* or *The Rock,* or any other action film. Lots of scenes going on.

The trend these days is lots of short, fast-paced scenes. Fifty or sixty years ago, it was longer, more developed scenes with a lot less "coverage" (different shots, angles, cuts). Look at old movies. Sometimes the camera was just set down in front of the players and left there for a five-minute scene. Sometimes this was done on purpose as an exercise in filmmaking, as Hitchcock did in Hume Cronyn's adaptation of Patrick Hamilton's play (screenplay by Arthur Laurents) *Rope.* Each scene was approximately ten minutes long (the length of a reel of film), and there are no readily discernable cuts (they're mostly hidden by camera moves). The action also takes place in real time. Now *there's* a challenge for you.

In other words, there is no one answer to this question. Most scenes take a couple of minutes to unfold. That would mean fifteen to twenty scenes in an act. Could be more, could be less. Depends. Just so long as they are all necessary. And you have all the necessary scenes.

WHOSE WORLD IS IT ANYWAY?

One of the great things about writing for film and television is that you get to order the chaos your way. One of the difficult things is to create your own world so that it is consistent. You have choices to make about what world you want your characters to inhabit—it could be the wild west of the 1870s, it could be the Midwest of the 1950s, it could be (and this is the easiest) Los Angeles of the first decades of the twenty-first century. All these worlds are real and researchable. But you can fly off from there and create the *Wild Wild West* of the 1870s, the *Back to the Future* of the '50s, *Iron Man* of the year 2008, or *Barbie* of the year 2023. Lots of worlds to create, and you can make your own rules in many of them, particularly in science fiction. But once you've created the rules, and the characters, you must be consistent. The rules must always apply. The apple always falls from the tree. You can't say "Except when it doesn't." Unless you've created a world without gravity. Then things are going to be different.

And I hope you have a damn good reason for it.

One of the things that will always spoil a movie for me is an action by a character that's just not plausible. I don't want to be thinking, "They set up that guy as an animal lover. Why did he kick his dog?" Unless that's important as a plot point, unless acting out of character was important, kicking his dog is going to make me think, "Didn't anyone pay attention here? He'd never kick his dog." I hate to say it, but those clichéd words that often emanate from an actor's mouth—"my character wouldn't say this"—can sometimes be true.

So be true to your character. Be true to your world. If you want to be true to your school, that's up to you.

Being consistent doesn't mean you can't be surprising. As long as your character's actions are logical within the framework you've set up, a surprise now and again is a good thing. Twists are what keep your film interesting and memorable. Who can forget the surprise of *The Crying Game*? Remember Faye Dunaway's confession in *Chinatown*?

How about learning what really had happened to Bruce Willis in *The Sixth Sense*? (I'm not telling just in case you haven't seen these films.) All these surprises, shocking as some are, make perfect sense within the film. They come out of the characters and worlds the writers have created.

JUST BEAT IT

A beat sheet is a preliminary step to an outline or story. It is a shorthand sketch of your entire movie, with a sentence or two serving as a description of each beat or scene. Using the typical three-act structure, a beat sheet helps you develop the structure of the movie, helps you to see where all your scenes fit in, and helps you make sure you've got a fully developed story before you start writing. Some people like to develop a beat sheet using 3x5 index cards on which they've written a short description of a scene. They lay them out on a bulletin board or the floor and shuffle them until they get them in the order that makes most sense. Then they write up a beat sheet or go directly to a treatment.

Whatever way you do it, the main thing to remember is the journey of your central character. How do we learn who they are? How do we find out what they want? How do they go about getting it? What do they confront along the way? What makes them change direction in the plot and in their character? Do the beats you've laid out show a gradual change in them as well as an exciting story? Is there a satisfying conclusion?

Now, when all those questions are answered, you order the beats and examine them more closely. Is each one necessary? Does each one make sense in the story? Can I do without it? Do I need to lay in something earlier that will pay off later? And the opposite: Have I paid off everything I've laid in?

A beginning, a middle, and an end. A person who goes through a test of character and comes out better. A story that moves forward constantly, that is logical but has surprises and has a satisfying conclusion.

If it were easy to do, you'd have learned it in high school. But it's also not impossible. About 250–300 feature films are made in the US each year, not including movies for streamers and first films from obscure new directors and writers. So, people do it. And they do it step by step, beat by beat, word by word.

Assignment

1. Read the sample beat sheet for *In Good Company*, screenplay by Paul Weitz (see page 41).
2. Write a beat sheet for your story, tracking the main character's arc.
3. Remember that beat sheets are malleable. You can change the order of the scenes, you can cut scenes, you can add scenes. If you discuss beat sheets in your writers group, acknowledge the strong points of the stories and then discuss what could make them better.

In Good Company

BEATS SUMMARIZED BY PAUL CHITLIK

ORDINARY LIFE

1. Dan Foreman goes through the ordinary morning routine and finds out from the news that his magazine has been bought by Teddy K.
2. He also discovers an empty pregnancy test box and thinks his daughter might be pregnant.
3. Dan visits one of his biggest clients, but the client decides to pull his advertising from Dan's magazine.
4. Carter Duryea presents a new marketing strategy for dinosaur phones just as his boss announces he's leaving to head up marketing at the magazine Teddy K has bought. Carter asks to be taken along, and he is.
5. Dan returns home and tries to get his daughter to open up to him (about possible pregnancy).
6. Dan goes to bed, but his wife is up. He asks about his daughter, Alex. But his wife tells him she's pregnant. Though he can't believe it at first, he's happy.
7. Carter is excited about his new job, etc., but his wife wants him to shut up and go to sleep. She questions his qualifications for the new job.
8. Others in Dan's office worry they're going to get fired. Dan gets demoted, his job taken by Carter.
9. Carter and Alex meet in the magazine's elevator. He confesses that he doesn't know what he's doing. She likes that.

INCITING INCIDENT (SEQUENCE)

10. In the office, Dan bumps into Carter by accident. Instead of staying, Dan goes to play tennis with Alex.
11. In an age-versus-youth match, Alex kicks his butt. Then she tells him she's transferring to NYU and will live in the city. Though it's going to be difficult, he agrees to the increased expense.
12. Carter is shown around the office, then shown his office—it's Dan's.
13. Dan returns to find him there. Carter's 26 and he's Dan's new boss. Dan responds by throwing a baseball at a trophy after Carter leaves.
14. The name plates are changed on the office door, and the employees switch offices.
15. Carter buys a new Porsche. He immediately gets into an accident.
16. When he gets home, his wife leaves him.
17. At the obstetrician's office, Dan has an attack of arrythmia and tells his wife, Ann, for the first time that he's been demoted.
18. Carter spends the night in his new car after a fast-food meal.

END OF ACT I

19. After downing a couple of lattes, Carter has trouble leading a sales meeting. But he comes up with an idea to synergize the sales force and increase sales by 20 percent (his goal).

ACT II

20. Carter takes Dan to a sushi restaurant and forces some sushi on him. He offers him the job of being his "wingman," though Dan doesn't see the merit of that. However, if he takes the position, he'll keep his job.

21. The first man Carter fires is the office kiss-up, who leaves angrily.
22. Carter shows himself to be a lonely workaholic in a series of shots. In one, he puts Dan down at a meeting.
23. Before the meeting, Carter's boss comes and tells Carter he's got to fire some more people. Carter's not happy about it.
24. As the meeting breaks up, Carter desperately tries to get someone to go for a drink with him, but no takers. Inadvertently, Dan invites him to dinner.
25. Carter is ecstatic to be there, but he makes a bad impression on Ann. Dan just wants to get rid of him. Dan and Ann discuss how they're going to meet the new college expenses.
26. Carter meets Alex in the living room. She's somewhat hostile. He admits that it's the anniversary of his first date with his wife. His honesty impresses her.
27. In the kitchen, Ann and Dan argue about Alex at NYU, then Dan drops the ziti on the floor and Ann pukes.
28. Alex and Carter play foosball and talk about peaking too early.
29. The pizza arrives and Dan gets his younger daughter off the phone. Dan calls Alex and Carter, the "kids," in for dinner.
30. At the table, there's some embarrassing conversation, and then Carter spills his drink into Dan's lap. Carter and Alex share a moment.
31. Carter reluctantly leaves, and Alex watches from the window.
32. Alone at his house, Carter feels alone.
33. Dan helps Alex move to the dorm at NYU.
34. Carter moves to a new apartment in the city.
35. Dan says goodbye to Alex after giving her pepper spray. He struggles to hold back the tears.

36. In matching scenes, Ann and Dan sign mortgage papers while Carter signs divorce papers.
37. Carter forces Dan to take some clients to the corporate box at a concert instead of a game and tells him he has to sell more pages or some people will be let go. They disagree on the use of the term "let go."
38. At the concert, the client is uncomfortable with the atmosphere but good with Dan. When they sneak out, the client informs him that his mega-corp is feuding with Dan's mega-corp, and he can't do business with Dan anymore.
39. Carter tells Dan he has to fire Louie and Morty . . . or himself.
40. Dan goes home to his family, and Carter sleeps on the couch at work.
41. Dan fires Morty and Louie. They don't take it well.
42. Dan turns in his own evaluation. He doesn't meet expectations.
43. Morty and Louie leave the office. Everyone's sad.

MIDPOINT

44. Carter bumps into Alex at an outdoor café. He has coffee with her. They hit it off and go for a walk.
45. They spend the day, and she invites him to her dorm room after kissing him.
46. Alex seduces a reluctant (again) Carter, and he succumbs.
47. In the office the next morning, Dan calls him jumpy, but Carter denies it.
48. In a montage, Alex and Carter play tennis, go out for coffee, etc. Carter fires more people. Dan tries calling Alex between shopping trips.

49. In an intramural basketball match, Dan meets Carter's boss, Mark, who's a jerk. There's a ringer on Mark's team. It's a rough game, and Dan gets injured in a dunk attempt.
50. Dan has concerns about getting in touch with his daughter, which Carter allays. Carter asks Dan for advice on keeping a marriage going.
51. Dan's family surprises him with a birthday party. He takes a minute to enter, then comes in wearing only his boxers. Surprise!
52. Dan talks to Morty, who isn't doing well, though his wife got a raise.
53. Carter meets with Alex in his car. He gives her an expensive necklace and tells her she's the kind of girl who it's good to be in a foxhole with (harkening to advice Dan had given him).
54. Later, opening his gifts, Dan discovers that Carter and Alex are together.

LOW POINT

55. Dan follows Carter to a restaurant and finds him there with Alex. He slugs him in a confrontation and has words with his daughter.
56. Carter goes to Alex's dorm, but she breaks up with him.

ACT III

57. When Dan returns home, he finds that Ann is in the hospital. He goes there, but it was just a scare about the baby.
58. At the hospital, Alex and Dan make up. She tells him he doesn't have to change, but he maintains that he does.
59. At the office, Teddy K shares his vision of the future with everyone. Dan challenges his thinking to his face. Teddy K leaves it to Dan and the others to answer Dan's questions.

A STORY LOW POINT

60. Mark storms into Dan's office and fires him. Carter resigns, too, but tells him he'll call Teddy K to tell him how Mark's driven the magazine into the ground. They get a short reprieve.

FINAL CHALLENGE

61. Dan and Carter visit a client and convince him to make a major ad buy in the magazine.
62. When they return, they find that Teddy K has sold the company to a rival. Mark and Carter lose their jobs, but Dan gets his old one back.
63. As Dan moves back into his office, Carter walks the streets, thinking.

RETURN TO THE (NOW CHANGED FOREVER) NORMAL LIFE

64. Carter returns to the office a month later in sweats and goes to see Dan. Carter turns down Dan's offer to come back to work as his second-in-command but acknowledges that Dan has done a lot for him. They part with a heartfelt hug.
65. At the elevator, Carter bumps into Alex, who's coming to play tennis with Dan. They have a tense conversation in front of Morty, who reminds them that timing is everything.
66. Dan announces to his daughters that they have a baby sister. He's "psyched."
67. Carter gets a call from Dan while jogging outside at the beach. They talk like old friends.

Lesson Five

WORD CHOICE MATTERS

In the world of motion pictures there are a lot of words for what we as writers do and for what we produce. Many times, executives will avoid the use of the verb "to write" and use something else to describe an activity that they want you to do. They do this because they don't want to acknowledge the process, nor the difficulty of the process. Or they're trying to get out of a payment triggered by asking for certain kinds of work. For example, which sounds tougher to do: "Take another pass at it" or "Do a complete rewrite"? How about "potchke" (a Yiddish word meaning *to fool around with*) or "rewrite?" Which sounds like more work: "Just lay out a couple of beats" or "Write an outline"?

I encourage you to use the words *write* and *create* as frequently as you can whenever talking to an executive.

That said, there are some words that writers (sometimes incorrectly) use interchangeably. A beat sheet, as described in the last lesson, can sometimes be called an outline. Then again, an outline can be called a treatment. Fortunately, a treatment can't be called a beat sheet. Why the confusion? No, it's not a conspiracy among executives but merely a degree of understanding as to what is expected.

A beat sheet lists, in the simplest of terms possible, the individual beats (scenes or parts of scenes) of a film. The plot points should be clear.

An outline (By the way, this word does not appear in the WGAW Schedule of Minimums, so officially there is no payment for this thing; remember that.) has the beats and a little more meat on the bone. The characters should be more fleshed out and the scenes described broadly.

A treatment can, and should, present all the beats, characterizations, bits of dialogue, and action of a film, so that we have a clear understanding of every step of the way. It should almost all be there. The film should be described in detail. This is also called "the story," and both words appear in the WGAW Schedule of Minimums and are used interchangeably there. This is a step you get paid for.

But there is still lots of confusion in the middle. I don't use the word *outline* as a general rule just to avoid confusion. I want my executives to know what to expect. If I say beat sheet (and sometimes I do as a preliminary to writing a treatment), it's clear. If I say treatment, it's clear. If I say outline, it's not.

SCENIC VIEW

As with everything else in writing, for the screen or otherwise, there are as many ways to write a scene as there are writers. That means good as well as bad. That means easy as well as difficult. That means I have some ideas on this subject, but they're not gospel; and to make things more complicated, I'm always changing them. But for now, here's how I suggest you do it.

I've already talked about the scene having a beginning, a middle, and an end. About it having conflict. Now let's talk about the course of that conflict and where we are in it when we enter and leave the scene, and why we're in it in the first place.

We know already that every major player in a scene has an objective—they want something. Usually, they want something different. Hence the conflict. We must also know what the emotion of that character is at the beginning of the scene, what their attitude is, what their long-term goal is. There's a helluva difference between a scene that starts off with everyone pissed off at each other from the get-go and one that starts with laughter. If you know your characters, you'll know what their emotions are at the beginning of the scene—are they happy, sad, angry?—and what will happen to them during the scene. Unless they have cause to change (they may or may not), they should maintain that emotion throughout the scene. Actors look at scenes this way (or the good ones do), and they look for hints the writer has given them.

We also need to know what the subject and purpose of the scene is. Yes, it's to move the story forward, first and foremost. But it may also be to shed some light on a character, to reveal information, to provide an obstacle. Know what you want to get across with your scene.

Now, where does your scene start? Okay, it starts at the beginning. No, it *has* a beginning, it doesn't necessarily *start* in the beginning. It should, in fact, start as late into the scene as possible and end as soon as it has an ending (not necessarily at the end of the scene). What do I mean by this? Let's take a domestic fight: say, for example, between Romeo and Juliet had they lived through that little misunderstanding about the poison. Romeo has a dead-end job at a supermarket packing bags. Juliet's got a kid at her breast and one on the way (it's possible, ask your OB-GYN). Romeo has been dressed down by the produce manager, and he's pissed. Where do we start the argument over dinner not being ready (which is really an argument about him having to be a wage slave and her having no one to talk to all day)? We could start it when he slams the door on entry to their stifling one-bedroom, un-air-conditioned hell-hole in North Hollywood. We could start it when he sees her lying on the couch flipping through channels with the remote. Or we could wait until he sits down at the table (not set for dinner) and starts pounding his fists. All, actually, good starting points, depending on the ending point you have in mind. I vote for the fists banging on the table.

Where do we end this revelation of domestic bliss that confronts teenagers who get married on impulse? If we had started it when the door slammed, we could have ended it at the fists hitting the table. If we start it at the fists hitting the table, we can end it when he throws the dish of spaghetti (again?!) to the floor, or when he clips her one, or when he stomps out the door. You decide. It depends on what you want to say about Romeo and Juliet, where you are in the movie, what their emotions are, where you started the scene in the first place. I'd end it before he leaves the house—we've seen that, and we know he's going to leave. But that's me. I like shorthand in my movies.

OBSTACLES AND TWISTS

If the road is easy, it's not interesting. Ever take the I-5 north from Los Angeles? Straight as an arrow to Sacramento. Hardly any scenery, no bends, no curves, just mind-numbing directness from point A to point B. You make a movie like that, and you know which way Ebert's thumb is going to point. Now, take Route 1 up the coast from LA. Cruise through the hills of Malibu, slow down through the twists and turns of Big Sur, drive through Carmel. It's a whole different world. Worth the trip for the journey itself. No one drives I-5 for fun. They do Route 1. (Unless they take the I-5 because they want to open up that Ferrari and see what it'll do on a straightaway until CHP sets up a roadblock. You can have fun with a VW Bug in Big Sur.)

What's a twist? Say Juliet was waiting to tell Romeo she's got another man. Say dinner's on the table and it's steak. Say the baby died. Say she won the lottery. Say she's waiting for him in a feather boa and nothing else. Say she's not even there when he gets home. All of these will spin your story off in another direction. All will make that scene a little different, more interesting, less clichéd. Don't do the obvious, just the logical. Every time your protagonist overcomes an obstacle, give them another, different one to overcome. Be as surprising as possible. Just make sure it makes sense within the context of the world you've established.

EMOTION

And lots of it. That's what a film should have. It's good to have an intellectual theme (and haven't I stressed that?). It's good to have great characters (where would *Star Wars* be without them?). It's good to have interesting locales, great ideas, and clever dialogue, but what really makes a movie is the quality of emotion it can stimulate. If your audience (or reader) isn't moved, doesn't laugh, isn't scared, what the hell are you doing it for anyway?

Okay, just a little rant on what's missing from films that seem to have all the elements, yet don't leave any impression on me. I want yours to be about something, about some*body*, and I want them to move me in some way. Doesn't mean I have to cry, doesn't mean I have to laugh out loud, but it does mean I have to feel something other than relief when I turn the last page. Think about in how many movies you just sit there waiting to be over. Too many. Think about ones that manipulate your emotions. (Try the ending of *Saving Private Ryan* if you're not sure what I'm talking about.) You remember the latter and forget the former.

How do you get emotion into your work? By feeling emotion when you write. By being deeply involved with your characters and by letting them have deep emotions in your scenes. How do you get people to laugh? By having the funny stuff come from the characters, not jokes they tell or clever lines (though that can sometimes help). What's funnier, Woody Allen talking to the audience, telling a joke he heard, or the lobster-cooking scene in *Annie Hall*?

Okay, it's not easy being emotional—sad, mad, elated, or funny. No one who's not a writer really understands how hard it is to be successful at putting emotions into words. But it's what ya gotta do.

THE TREATMENT

There are two ways to write treatments—the industry way and my way. Actually, my way is just a slight amendment to the industry way. Here it is: Describe every character and every scene in prose, let me know where the end of each act is, and do it in about twenty pages or so. Throw in bits of dialogue, jokes if you have them, all the twists and turns, all the supporting characters, how each scene begins and how it ends, everything. Okay, it may take up to thirty pages. American

Playhouse once asked for a document (only word for it at that time) from me and my then writing partner, Jeremy Finch, that had everything. I mean *everything*. It was sixty pages long, double spaced, no cheating on the margins. We basically reformatted it and had a script ready in about an hour. Okay, that's an exaggeration, but we sure knew where we were going when we sat down to write the teleplay.

If you've got a good beat sheet or a nice set of index cards with your scenes sketched out, you should be able to write a treatment from either of them without tearing out your hair. (Until you get to a part that doesn't work because, well, the characters changed their minds, or you came up with something great right in the middle, or you forgot something when you wrote out the cards.) The process can be nerve-wracking, but a good treatment is more than half the work on a film, in my estimation.

So that's what I want you to begin this week. And remember, it's only the first draft. Not only is it unlikely to be perfect, it shouldn't be perfect. So don't not turn it in because it's not "perfect." Rewriting is going to be required anyway. Just get some words on paper. That's what writers do. You'll change them maybe a hundred times, but you can't rewrite unless you write. And you can't call yourself a writer unless you write.

It's all in there. Now, just get it down on paper and have a look at it.

Assignment

1. Read treatments for *Goddess of Fury* and *The Bike Brigade*. (Used with permission of the author. See pages 53 and 71.)
2. Revise and expand the first half of your beat sheet to include full description of scenes. In other words, write the first half of your treatment.
3. Watch *Thelma & Louise*.
4. If you're in a writers group, rather than read all the other beat sheets, pair up and read only one other. (If you have the time to read more, great.) Give feedback on the stories in the same way you'd like to hear feedback on your own story. The goal is to improve the story at each stage.

Treatment for *Goddess of Fury*

Written by Martín Olmedo

From the outside it looks like the most crowded train in the world, with people riding on top of the cars, hanging out the windows, standing in the spaces between the cars as it crosses the Indian subcontinent in 1912. It whistles as it draws near a bend.

Men with guns and rifles wait on the rocks. From their hiding place, others start galloping alongside the tracks as they hear the train coming.

Inside, a comfortable first-class compartment with just a few Anglo travelers, including Jane Winters, 28, wearing a blouse and a pair of riding pants—a little daring for her time. She carries on a terse conversation with Miss Julia Leverton, late 50s, a somewhat large and prissy woman in a long, and what must be uncomfortable, dress. "And what was the matter with Mr. Worthington?" Miss Leverton asks. "Too dull," Jane replies. "Mr. Venturelli?" "Too exciting." "Mr. Bougeron?" "Too old." "Mr. Steinmetz?" "Too young. Why are you so concerned all of the sudden that I haven't found a husband, or rather, that a husband hasn't found me?" Miss Leverton admits it doesn't really matter to her, except if Jane were married, it would be her husband traveling with Jane instead of her in this godforsaken country with all its . . . its Indians.

The men, a band of robbers, race alongside the train on horses, then leap onto the train from horseback and start to make their way through the cars towards first class.

Jane reminds Leverton she was the one that insisted she come to accompany her for the dedication of the museum named for her father. She thought it would be an invaluable opportunity for research. And to pay respect to her father and help her accept his death. Jane fingers a small necklace with the figure of Shiva on it—a present her father sent her when he was first in India, before he was killed in the monsoon. And, anyway, she's not interested in finding a husband, especially if you define a husband as someone who has a career and is able to support himself, be intellectually stimulating and able to protect his family. That pretty much describes her already.

The bandits make their way down the corridor, terrorizing everyone in their path, robbing them of their valuables, pushing them around. A couple of men try to stop them, and they're beaten unmercifully.

Jane says she needs a husband like a fish needs a bicycle. The only thing she can't do is vote, and that will change. "Oh, no, dear," Miss Leverton says, "they'll never let us vote."

Before Jane can respond, bandits burst into their compartment and demand all the passengers' valuables. Jane doesn't want to hand over their valuables, but Miss Leverton insists. Jane complies, but then one of the bandits rips the Shiva necklace from Jane's neck. Jane asks for it back, her anger controlled. Then she demands it. Then she karate kicks him down, grabs the necklace, then takes on the other bandit. The fight spills out into the aisle, then goes between cars as she takes on one after the other. The fight travels to the roof of the train and its pretty wild until a tunnel is spotted in the distance. Jane can't see it, and the bandit just tries to keep her standing. But at the last minute, she reverses positions with him, sees the tunnel, ducks in time, but he doesn't. On the other side of the tunnel, she gets up, the Shiva in her hand.

Back in the compartment, Miss Leverton brushes the dust off Jane. "Oh, look at you, you are a mess," she says. "It's good I was here to take care of things."

Jane and Miss Leverton arrive in Jaipur. There is no one to meet them at the teeming station. They push their way through pick-pockets, beggars, and guides. Jane catches one with his hand in her handbag. She pulls it out and holds the man in her grip until he releases what he was trying to steal. "Didn't your mother teach you to keep your hands to yourself?" she says, and she lets him go. He runs away. Another Indian man pushes to the front and introduces himself. He is Apu. Jane is suspicious. But Apu quickly explains that he's been sent by Captain Harrington to take them to the American consulate. He organizes a group of porters to take their luggage.

On the street, they make their way toward the American consulate. Jane and Miss Leverton ride in a carriage while Apu and the porters follow on foot. Jane is fascinated while Miss Leverton is disgusted by the crowds as they go through the marketplace.

At the consulate, Captain Harrington, late 30s, the military attaché, welcomes Jane and Miss Leverton. He's happy to see them again. It's been years since they met in San Francisco. He was a great admirer of her father. An English businessman, Thomas Nicholson, 30s, is shown in by Mr. Singh, Harrington's Indian assistant, about 50. Singh can't take his eyes off Miss Leverton, and though he says nothing, Leverton turns away shocked.

Nicholson's a friend of Harrington's and semi-official chamber of commerce head. He's good-looking and flirts with Jane, but Jane is more interested in knowing more about the village where her father died. Harrington and Nicholson say it's remote. No English ever go there. "My father did," Jane says. Nicholson asks if he can pick her up at the hotel and take Jane that evening for the museum naming, but Jane declines.

At the hotel, while Jane trains, Miss Leverton admonishes her for turning down Nicholson's invitation. He's a good marriage prospect. "You're too picky," Leverton says. "I'm not here to get involved, I'm here to honor my father," Jane tells her, but Miss Leverton insists that the boat has sailed for her and anytime a lifeline is thrown, she should take it. As Jane pounds a padded post with her hands and feet, she says she doesn't need a lifeline. Miss Leverton says she does—she knows how devastated Jane was when her father was killed. And since her mother died, she has no one. Jane says she has Miss Leverton, but Leverton, though touched, says it's not enough.

At the reception, there are speeches and a tour during which Nicholson tries to romance Jane, to the annoyance of Harrington. Nicholson tells her the cult of Kali is still active in the area her father last visited. Thinking he's going to scare her, he tells her it's a bloody cult that worships a goddess regularly involved in ritual killing and human sacrifices. She in turn tells Nicholson that the area is also the probable origin of martial arts now practiced in China, Japan, and even the US. Nicholson has never heard of martial arts. Does she mean fencing? No, she means Chinese boxing, Wing Chun, White Crane. Harrington explains—formal systems of hand-to-hand combat. They've been known in the US for years. Teddy Roosevelt studied Judo in the White House, though the current president, Taft, would fall on his ass if he tried a high kick.

Jane explains that in his zeal to trace the origins of martial arts, her father had traveled the world, starting in Greece, Persia, China, Japan, Okinawa. He felt that remote Indian villages had the purest form of martial arts, preserved since Alexander the Great brought them from Greece, as they were the most isolated. Nicholson is impressed that a woman would know so much about the topic. Jane thanks him for the compliment. The University of California paid her a similar one when it made her a professor in history there for continuing her father's work.

After the dedication ceremony, Jane is momentarily alone with Leverton as Nicholson and Harrington attend to some business. They're approached by an Indian man who hands Jane an obviously old letter. He disappears before she can ask any questions. Jane and Leverton find a quiet place and read the letter.

In the letter, her father apologizes to her for his long absence. He's sorry he hasn't been a better parent. He'll tell her all the details when he sees her again. Jane is thrilled that her father might still be alive. She's going to go to the village where he was last seen and investigate. Miss Leverton believes that would be a wild goose chase. Jane disagrees. They could find out what happened to him and, if possible, make sure he has a decent burial if he is, in fact, dead. Miss Leverton maintains that the letter is a hoax, written after Jane's father died in a flood caused by a monsoon over fifteen years ago. It's time she accepted what happened and moved on. There's nothing concrete to accept. But Jane asks, why would anyone forge such a document? She can't bear not knowing.

She's going for sure. She announces this to Nicholson and Harrington when they return. They're very skeptical of the veracity of the letter and even more skeptical about her chances of finding him alive, not to mention the dangers of traveling in the remotest parts of India.

But Jane wants to go there anyway. The men, and even Mr. Singh who has been accompanying Harrington, warn against it. There are many things there that would put her and Miss Leverton in danger, including the upcoming monsoon season. But Jane insists. She'll hire a guide and set off as soon as possible. They summon Apu, who is from the region. They assign him to accompany Jane and Miss Leverton. He doesn't want to return there, but they insist. They'll prepare to leave tomorrow.

Again, Nicholson warns her not to go. She insists she will. He flirts with her, but she ignores it. He warns her about the head of the cult, said to be ruthless. "More ruthless than an English businessman?" she says, taunting him. "Nothing is more ruthless than that," he laughs. Anyway, she's not worried, she's got Miss Leverton to protect her.

Harrington offers to accompany Jane on her way home, and they are attacked in the street by a band of men who try to steal the letter. Jane fights them and saves Harrington's life when two of the men are about to strangle him. He warns her to leave India, but she insists on continuing.

The next morning, when Jane opens the door to her hotel room, the man who gave her the letter is lying on the floor in the hall, strangled to death with a silk scarf. Jane is now more determined than ever to go on her quest, even though Leverton is scared shitless. Still, later that day, Jane, Miss Leverton, Apu, and the porters prepare to set off for the village via elephant and horse. Miss Leverton won't climb onto the elephant as she is afraid of heights. She makes Apu give up his horse, and he rides with Jane. Harrington brings them a brace of carrier pigeons just in case. He really is quite concerned. There is no telegraph where they're going, not to mention telephone. Miss Leverton thinks

Harrington's interested in Jane, but Jane doesn't see it. And if she did, she wouldn't care. She's still incapable of making any kind of long-term emotional attachments.

The road is rough, and the swaying of the elephants makes Jane a little green. That night they have a proper English high tea around the campfire. But there are lots of spooky noises. Miss Leverton is scared, especially when Apu tells them of the horrors of the Thugs. Jane thought they had been eliminated decades ago, but he assures them they had not. And they worship the goddess Kali, the consort of Shiva, the one she has around her throat. But Kali is evil, and she devours all that exists. Once, human sacrifices were made to her. That's why the Thugs are devoted to her. But Memsahib Jane has nothing to worry about from them, he explains, since they never strangle women. Or, at least, they never have up 'til now.

The next morning, there is a figure of Kali drawn with ashes from the fire. Apu wants to return to Jaipur, but they won't let him. He's really spooked when he discovers that three graves have been dug on the edge of the campsite. He explains that Thugs dig the graves of their intended victims before they murder them. He wants to leave. The porters threaten rebellion. Jane convinces him to accompany them only to the outskirts of the village. He needn't enter with them.

Later that morning, they reach a chasm and must leave the animals behind, since the only way across is a decrepit rope bridge. When the boards give way, they are forced to cross the bridge hand over hand, hanging from the ropes. Miss Leverton is emphatic! She won't go! The height scares her. But when Jane goes on ahead anyway, she won't be left behind. Despite a safety harness that Jane rigs for Miss Leverton, she nearly goes to the bottom of the gorge.

Later that day they are ambushed by a group of Thugs on the trail just outside the village. Apu and some of the porters are taken prisoner, while most of the others flee, but not before the pigeons have been accidentally released in a flurry of feathers. A few of the porters are pulled aside and strangled with scarves. Jane fights several of the attackers at a time, kicking, punching, and flipping them. But there are too many of them to fight. Jane grabs Miss Leverton, and they run toward the village. As they turn a corner in the scraggly trail, Jane trips and falls, tumbling over a cliff and landing on a narrow ledge. She yells for Leverton, but when she looks up, she sees the face of Robert Fitzsimmons, tall, late 30s, completely Indian looking now, deeply tanned, dressed in Indian clothes and a turban. He's scary from that angle but reaches down and helps her up. He'd be handsome if it weren't for the scar that goes down the left side of his face from the hairline to his chin, just barely missing his eye. He introduces himself as Jarwahal.

Jane doesn't recognize Fitzsimmons, her father's young assistant who also had been reported missing. But she's very happy to see him. And there are sparks between them. She tells him of the ambush, and he promises to send his guards to see what has happened to the others and to retrieve their things. He asks her why she is here, and she explains. He tells her he remembers her father well. He was a special man. He tells her that her father and his assistant were exploring an abandoned temple dedicated to the worship of Kali, the bloodthirsty consort of Shiva, in the jungle near the village. Jarwahal was, in fact, their guide. They had been told that art depicting martial arts combat could be found in the temple. A sudden monsoon brought a rainstorm that made the river overflow its banks, and they were caught in a flash flood. They were swept away in the current. Jarwahal tried to save them, but only he survived. Shortly after that, he, Jarwahal, vowed to end the flood danger in the village by building a dam.

He invites them to the ashram of Shiva where he has lived in prayer since that time. As they walk through the village, Jane sees that the villagers bow to him everywhere he goes. She asks why. He tells her that when he built the dam, it not only protected the village, but it made possible the expansion of a small gold mine that had supported the ashram. That led to the creation of many jobs for the village. Jane notes an unusual number of cripples and sick. Jarwahal blames their problems on their superstitions about modern medicine and their poor hygiene.

The ashram is dark and creepy. There are numerous figures of Shiva, but there are also cloths draped over other statues. There is lots of scurrying in the shadows of the ashram, and Miss Leverton would rather not stay there. But Jane convinces her it will be all right. In their quarters, Miss Leverton and Jane clean up and are given Indian clothes. Miss Leverton can't figure how to wear the sari and doesn't want to get tangled up in the cloth. A serving woman shows her how. As she's being wrapped in the sari by the serving woman, Miss Leverton tries to discourage Jane from starting a romance with Jarwahal. Jane can't believe this—she shows some interest in a man, and now Leverton wants her to drop it. "Well, he's Indian, don't you know." Jane says she'll have a romance with whomever she wants. It's just that she doesn't really want to right now. But the man does know a lot about her father. Maybe he can tell her more. Jane dismisses that idea. Then Miss Leverton wants to get out of this creepy place; there's no point in staying any longer. But Jane's not going anywhere until she learns the truth about her father. If Jarwahal was strong enough to grasp a statue to save his life, so was her father, who was in superb shape all his life. Jarwahal isn't telling all.

As Jane and Miss Leverton go to dinner, they walk by Jarwahal's library where he is weighing gold dust and entering a number in an account book. He sees them at the door and urges them to go ahead, he'll be with them in a minute.

That evening, Jarwahal hosts a ceremonial dinner at the ashram. There is Indian music and dance, which Miss Leverton comments on: "See, movement can be graceful. It doesn't have to be *ay yah!*, like your Chinese boxing." "Yes," Jane replied, "I could have danced my way out of the arms of the men who attacked us on the trail." Jane probes Jarwahal's story until he gets annoyed. He changes the subject and tells her about Kalari Payatt, the Indian martial art. She heard of this from her father and begs him for a demonstration, but he says no, it is not for women to see. It is sacred. Jane pushes, reminding him that Chinese boxing and Jiujitsu were also only for men, but her father and her Chinese mother trained her in both. He deftly changes the subject, offering to show them the mining operation in the morning.

While Jarwahal's attention is held by someone who has come to him, a serving woman whispers into Jane's ear. She says, "I must talk to you." She won't say why, but she shows them her ring—it was the professor's. She will tell them how she got it if they will meet with her. They agree to meet later that night. She will come to them. They must keep the meeting secret.

That night the woman comes to Jane and Miss Leverton's chambers. The woman explains that she was the professor's housekeeper. He gave her the ring when he ran out of money. It's clear she was devoted to the man. She must show them something. The woman leads them deep into the bowels of the ashram where they come out onto the balcony of a huge underground hall. In hiding, they observe some sort of religious ritual taking place. The leading priest has his back to them. Then they spot their guide, Apu, led into the hall in chains. He is released from the chains but confronted by a martial arts Thug. The fight is short, but fierce. Apu is fighting for his life, but he is no match for the Thug. He is knocked unconscious, then strangled with a scarf. His body is dumped into a sluice from the river and washed away. Then the leader turns to address the chanting congregation. It's Jarwahal! They hear someone coming and duck into the shadows behind a pillar. The man turns the other way, and they appear to be safe. But he has seen them.

On the way back, they pass Jarwahal/Fitz's library. Jane enters, leaving a scared Miss Leverton to be the lookout. She finds the account book that Jarwahal/Fitzsimmons had been working on earlier that day in a drawer. In it, she sees notations regarding the amount of gold taken and the amount of arsenic used in the mining operation. She explains to Miss Leverton that often arsenic or mercury is used in gold mining to separate the gold from the ore. Miss Leverton hears someone coming and signals to Jane, who hastily puts the book back in the drawer. But the drawer falls out and a notebook in a familiar handwriting falls out and opens in front of her. It's her father's lost notes on Indian martial arts—complete with drawings.

Miss Leverton tells her to hurry, someone's coming. Jane struggles to get the drawer back in, and it doesn't look like she's going to make it. Miss Leverton sees this and goes down the hall to waylay the guards. She flirts outrageously with them, but they just want to get by her. She tries fainting, but that only works for a second. Soon, they go by her and enter the library and retrieve something from the desktop. Jane is nowhere to be seen. But we see her under the desk. They come close to discovering her, but don't.

After they leave, Miss Leverton pokes her head in, and Jane comes out of hiding. She's got a lot to tell her.

The next morning Jane and Miss Leverton sneak out early. They meet up with the professor's housekeeper in the village, and she shows them how polluted the water is. There is foam on the river below the mines. Locals draw water from the river and bathe in it. Jane sees children drinking from it. She sees the sluice carrying water from the mine emptying into the river. She surmises that it must be carrying the arsenic used in separating the gold from the ore. The water must be poisonous, she tells the housekeeper, and several people overhear them. That's why there are dead fish lying on the banks of the river. This starts a panic. "The water is poisoned! The water is poisoned!" She asks the villagers why they don't destroy the sluice. They tell her they would die if they did.

Jane storms back to the ashram, determined to take this up with Jarwahal. On the way back to the ashram, they are attacked. The Indian woman is quickly separated from Jane and Miss Leverton in the fight, and they lose track of her. A few of Jarwahal's men come to their rescue and escort Jane and Miss Leverton into Jarwahal's chambers. They throw them into the room where Fitz/Jarwahal is eating breakfast. Fitz/Jarwahal apologizes for his servants' lack of manners. If they were rough, it is only because they were concerned about Jane and Miss Leverton's safety. The mob was ready to riot. It's dangerous for foreigners to walk unescorted in the village and say things that could get the locals excited. Jane asks him about the arsenic in the water, and he says it's nothing to worry her pretty little head about. She wonders how big a head a woman is supposed to have if hers is considered little.

Fitz/Jarwahal apologizes for his careless remark but adds that the arsenic is harmless in small quantities. It's even used in some medicines, after all. He chastises her for what happened in the village. It's not good to feed the locals mistruths. They could get unruly, and that would be bad . . . for everyone.

Outside, he proudly points to the dam he built after the monsoon in which her father died. It prevents flooding in the village for the first time in hundreds of years. Isn't that a good thing? It also made it possible for him to build the sluice that directs water into the mine. A few remaining traders from the East India Trading Company help him sell the gold. He pours the proceeds into the development of the temple and the village. Jane and Miss Leverton pretend to be happy with his explanation. He invites Jane to a special quiet dinner that night when he can tell her of his other plans for the development of the village and share stories about her father. He requests that Miss Leverton dine with his staff. Highly insulted, Miss Leverton objects to that at first, but after a signal from Jane, she accepts.

Later, as they prepare Jane for the dinner, they see several men carrying a shrouded body through the courtyard several stories below. They can't see who the person is, but a hand slips out of the shroud. It's got the professor's ring on it! Miss Leverton insists they've got to get out of here now! Jarwahal is going to catch on that they know about the extent of the pollution and that he's the leader of the cult. They're not safe. Jane argues that she needs to know more about what happened to her father. Leverton objects: "Look what they did to this woman. They could do it to us." Jane insists that they stay, but she sees Miss Leverton's fear and concedes that this will be their last night here.

At the dinner, Fitz/Jarwahal is very seductive. He tells her that the villagers think he's immortal, and he just may be. He's set for life here. He takes her hand and tells her there is only one thing missing in his life. Then he asks her to be his wife. He's been waiting all his life for a woman like her. There's no one in the village to compare. She turns him down gently, but he reacts badly, saying she'll be sorry. Now, he can't let her leave here. He knows she saw the ceremony last night. He's going to have to take care of her like he took care of her father. He signals for his Thugs to take her away, but before they can grab her, she goes into a fighting stance. They attempt to grab her, but she fights them until Fitzsimmons/Jarwahal grabs her from the back, applying enough pressure to paralyze her momentarily.

As the men bind her, Fitzsimmons/Jarwahal tells her the professor was treated like a god when he arrived: Local legend held that a great fighter would come to the village to take his place on the throne of Kali. Because he knew martial arts, Professor Winters was thought to be that man. The villagers would have done anything for him. But he wasn't interested in that. He left Fitzsimmons to watch things while he went to other, even more remote villages to search for the origins of Kalari Payatt, the mother of all martial arts. Him? Yes, him. He is Fitzsimmons. Instantly Jane knows he killed her father. Fitz goes on with his story. He liked the power. He discovered the mine that had been supporting the cult modestly. He expanded it.

When Professor Winters returned, he didn't agree with some of the changes Fitz had made. "Necessary changes," like intimidating the villagers with threats of death from the Thugs. He thought Fitz had gone too far when really he hadn't yet gone far enough in bending the locals to his will. The professor belittled him, saying he wanted nothing more to do with him. He told him to leave the village. But the professor had underestimated Fitz. Fitz locked the professor up. He kept him drugged to show the people their "god" from time to time until his own power was cemented. He also threatened to have Thugs find and kill Jane in the US. Her father lived for a time as a virtual slave. Finally, he could bear no more. He tried to escape and got as far as the closest train station. Instead of a train, he caught a silk scarf around the neck in the traditional execution method of the Thugs.

Now Fitz will have to devise something different for her since his men are forbidden by their religion to use silk scarves on women. But he's sure they'll find something appropriate. All that remains is to dig the graves. He'll have them dug next to her father's in the courtyard. She's taken back to her quarters by two hefty guards, but she struggles out of her bindings on the way back and tries to escape. They catch her, and though they're beaten pretty badly by her, they overpower her and throw her back into her chambers.

Jane looks for a way out of their chambers, but they're several stories up and their windows lead to a straight drop. But Miss Leverton has an idea—she ties several saris together and attaches them to the bed. She drops them out the window and beckons for Jane to climb down. Jane says she's crazy. They'll get killed in the fall. And, besides, isn't Miss Leverton afraid of heights? "That was then, this is now," Miss Leverton says as she climbs out the window and takes hold of the saris. She says, "God hates a coward," and she's gone.

They flee from the village, running as fast as they can. They round a bend through a pass and run right into Nicholson on his way to the village. They're saved. But, no, he surprises them and forces them to return to Fitz at gunpoint. When the women ask him why he's holding them, he tells them he doesn't want to stop the flow of gold that goes through him.

Nicholson brings his captives to Fitz. He apologizes that Captain Harrison didn't do his job and keep the women in Jaipur. He should be disciplined or eliminated. There doesn't seem to be any integrity to the system of payoffs like there once was. He just took their money and ignored their orders. He apologizes to Jane. He's never going to be able to show her the town now. Fitz barks an order to his men, the same two from whom she nearly escaped, and the women are hustled away roughly.

Jane and Miss Leverton are thrown into a cell with unruly villagers starved for female companionship. They try to rape her and Miss Leverton. She subdues them. Later, they hear noises and look out their windows. They see a pair of Thugs using pickaxes to dig shallow graves in the courtyard of the ashram.

Nicholson and Fitz examine the next shipment of gold. Nicholson gives Fitz a bank receipt from the last deposit he transported to the city for him and asks him when he will have enough. He's already a millionaire many times over. Fitz says it isn't the money any longer. Where else could he enjoy this power over life and death? Nicholson says he must control himself—killing a few Indians here and there is one thing, but does he really have to kill these women? There'll be lots of questions from Harrington that he would rather not answer. Fitz tells him the gold will supply the answers for him and not to worry.

Back in the cell, Miss Leverton lures the guard to the cell door and Jane grabs him by the neck, puts her other hand on his mouth, and knocks him out cold. They grab the keys, but they're discovered by other guards as they're leaving the cell. They have to fight their way out. At one stage it looks like Jane is in too deep with a pair of Thugs, but Miss Leverton knocks one of them out from behind.

Jane wants to retrieve her father's writings, bring Fitz to justice, and help the villagers, but Miss Leverton just wants to escape. She can feel the monsoon wind that brings the rains. But Jane heads for the library to get the notebook, and Miss Leverton has no choice but to follow. They race down the halls as the hubbub from the dungeons rises up. In the library, they grab the professor's notebook and fly out the front door.

In the town square, Jane tries to convince the people to take action and destroy the sluice that goes into the mine, but they're scared. They don't want to do anything to anger Fitz. They believe he is immortal. He would have them killed. Just then, a drop of rain falls on Miss Leverton's face. "Uh-oh." The monsoon is arriving. One drop turns into hundreds. Then Fitz appears in the square, followed by Nicholson. The crowd hushes. He sets several of his men on Jane, who throws the notebook to Miss Leverton and defends herself using all of her martial arts expertise. The crowd is stunned. They've never seen a woman defending herself like this. She fights off several of Fitz's men, and then Fitz calls them off. He's hers. They circle each other cautiously. Finally, he attacks, but she draws first blood. The villagers are stunned to see this woman expose this alleged god's mortality.

The rain is coming down hard now, and Jane urges the villagers to destroy the sluice, but Fitz pulls a sword and threatens the villagers with death if anyone takes a step. Jane kicks the sword out of his hand, and they fight as the villagers storm the sluice.

The fight travels into the temple of Kali. The showdown between Jane and Fitz goes back and forth. He tells her he'll crush her like he crushed her father, but that only stirs her on to try harder.

She beats him on the steps of the altar. When she emerges alone from the temple, the monsoon suddenly stops. The villagers have destroyed the sluice and saved the dam.

It's over. Jane walks through the crowd, which separates for her. Some of them get on their knees and call to her as if she were a goddess herself. They appear fearful, as they did before Fitz. She pulls them to their feet as she walks. As she leaves the grateful crowd, she sees Harrington arrive leading some British soldiers, led by Miss Leverton. They've got Nicholson under arrest. They had received the pigeons with no message, so they decided to come. They had to leave the horses at the chasm, so they were slowed down, but "no harm done, eh?" Harrington asks.

A funeral pyre at night. Jane and Miss Leverton are in saris. Harrington and his aide, Mr. Singh, are in dress uniform. Local villagers gather around and chant as the professor's body, wrapped in a shroud, is commended to the fire. Mr. Singh smiles at Miss Leverton, who smiles back. Singh says, "Perhaps we will meet again." She says, "I've always thought India was a lovely country." Jane turns to Miss Leverton. "My father's work isn't completed. Perhaps I can take a leave of absence, stay here and finish it, and kill two birds with one stone." She winks at Miss Leverton as she takes Harrington's arm, and they walk away from the fire.

THE END

Treatment for *The Bike Brigade*

Written by Martín Olmedo

(A shorter treatment for a shorter film for children.)

ACT I

RYAN BURKE, 13, small but wiry, and his mom, BETH, drive along a country road with his golden retriever, JUPITER, toward the small city where his father lives. While Jupiter chews on a squeaky toy, Ryan complains about having to stay with Dad for the summer. Mom reminds him he hasn't seen his father since spring vacation and that it's Dad's turn to have him for the summer—court order. Ryan hates living with his father, who's always so busy. He hates being away from his friends. Mom points out that he doesn't have that many friends. Ryan hugs his dog and says at least he has Jupiter, his best friend. He's the only one he can count on since his brother Brandon died. The car pulls to a stop in front of Dad's house.

Seeing Dad is awkward. They haven't spoken much lately. Mom and Dad immediately start negotiating pickup dates and other issues, so Ryan goes into the house, practically without speaking to Dad (NED). Then Mom and Dad argue about leaving the dog. Dad doesn't want him—he's a pain in the neck. But Mom takes off, leaving him holding the leash.

The next morning, a Sunday, Ryan expects to spend some time with Dad, but Dad's got some work he needs to take care of first. Ryan's not surprised. He wanders out to explore the backyard and discovers Brandon's old bicycle in the garage. Dad comes out to look for him later and offers his help to fix the bike up. Not now, of course, he's busy. But when he's done. But Ryan refuses. He doesn't want to have to wait until Christmas to fix up the bike. They have a few words about it, and Ryan ends up fixing the bike on his own with Jupiter at his side. When it's rideable, he does a little bike dancing. Then he takes it out for a spin. He leaves Jupiter behind and forgets to close the gate.

Not far from his house, he discovers an undeveloped piece of land with some narrow bike trails. He's zooming down a trail when a group of kids on bikes whizzes by him, causing him to run off the trail and into a bush. The kids, KYLE, 13, LISA HARRINGTON, 12, and CARLOS, 13, laugh, then take off. Ryan's more embarrassed than hurt.

Meanwhile, a pair of trying-to-be-tough guys, EARL, 20s, and PERCY, late 20s, cruise the streets in a beat-up old van. There are two or three dogs in the back of the van in small kennels barking their heads off. Earl comments that he likes the hours of this job but can't stand the noise. Percy digs the money, and it's only going to get better. But Earl complains he's going to lose his hearing and end up like Rush Limbaugh if this keeps up. Percy has no clue as to who Rush is. Doesn't matter. "Look for dogs, we're two short of our quota for the day."

Back at the house, Jupiter wanders out of the yard and into the street. He looks up the street, down the street. Where's Ryan? He lopes down the street just as Earl and Percy cruise by in the van. They pull up to the curb a little ahead of Jupiter, jump out, and lure him into the van with a squeaky toy.

When Ryan gets home, Dad is there with his girlfriend, GAIL, and Gail's son, Kyle—the one from the group of the kids who had run Ryan off the trail. They pretend they haven't met, but the relationship is strained. Ryan quickly excuses himself—it's time to feed

Jupiter. But when Ryan goes into the backyard, Jupiter doesn't answer to his whistle. He's gone.

Earl and Percy unload the dogs at a testing laboratory on the outskirts of the city. Their boss, STAN, who has the contract with the lab to provide the dogs, meets them at the back door. Earl doesn't like being a dog catcher, but the provider reminds him the dogs are worth $100 each to them. Stan says the lab has ordered more dogs for their experiments regarding muscle function and strokes. They need big, strong dogs. The weak ones will be put down—and they get no money for those. Earl and Percy sort the dogs, commenting on Jupiter as a good example. They have trouble managing the other dogs and get tangled up in leashes. The barking is deafening, and they have to yell at each other.

Dad is sure Jupiter will come back, but Ryan points out that the dog doesn't know the neighborhood and won't be able to find his way. Kyle offers to help him find Jupiter, but Ryan says it was his fault; it's his responsibility to find him.

Ryan rides around the neighborhood but finds nothing. It's too dark. He practically gets hit by Earl and Percy's van on their way home from work.

ACT II

The next morning Kyle, (Lisa) Harrington, and Carlos meet out on the trail. When Harrington hears that Ryan's dog is missing, she says they've got to help. She'd feel terrible if her own dog, King, were stolen, so she knows how Ryan feels. Kyle understands, too. He has a dog as well. They agree to go out and look for Jupiter. They find Ryan searching the streets, and they join up with him. At first, he refuses help, but Harrington pleads. Harrington and

Ryan share a look, and Ryan reluctantly accepts. Harrington asks for a picture of the dog.

Later that day, Harrington brings over a poster with Jupiter's picture on it. Harrington tells Ryan the posters might jog someone's memory. At least make people aware that Jupiter's missing. Ryan gives her a big smile. They all distribute the poster on their bikes.

Ryan's dad, Ned, reminds Ryan that Jupiter's just a dog. He should accept that Jupiter may be gone. Ryan won't. Dad doesn't understand that Jupiter's more than a dog. He's family. And Jupiter's all he has left from his brother, Brandon. Jupiter's always been there for him. He has to be there for Jupiter.

In a montage, we see the Brigade hand out their flyers to various people who shake their heads no.

At the animal shelter, Ryan and Harrington talk to the animal control officer. He says he hasn't seen a dog like Jupiter. He's sorry. They should check back every couple of days, though. When they leave, he makes a phone call: "Hello, Earl?"

Ryan and Kyle distribute flyers at a pet store. The store owner asks if they've checked the pound. They have. Before they leave, a customer tells them how dognappers pick up dogs from the street and sell them to labs that use the dogs for experiments. He also tells them how the dognappers sometimes find dogs listed in the newspaper as "lost" and claim to be their owners. Then they sell the dogs at the labs. It's one thing to experiment on animals, it's another to experiment on pets that are practically like people themselves. And it's theft. Carlos maintains dogs are not like people, that the research helps thousands of humans. Ryan tells Carlos he doesn't know what he's talking about. Jupiter is his best friend. More like "people" than he (Carlos) is. They get a little mad, maybe even shove each other a little, and Harrington and Kyle have to break them up.

Ryan is horrified. He's got to find Jupiter before anything happens to him. Why not pretend we found a dog and put an ad in the paper, Harrington suggests. Then maybe the dognappers will come to claim it, and we can see who they are. They immediately call an ad into the local newspaper claiming they've found a lost dog. They use Harrington's phone number.

The next morning, Ryan checks the paper. Their ad's in it. He bails out of his breakfast, and, before his father can object, he rushes off to Harrington's house to wait for the dognappers to call. Ryan and Harrington talk. She tells him to take the chip off his shoulder. Let people be his friend. The others arrive, excited about the ad. Harrington whispers with Kyle and Carlos. Kyle nods his head; Carlos shakes his. She whispers some more. Finally, Carlos agrees. Harrington tells Ryan they're going to make him a member of the Bike Brigade, their biking club.

Earl and Percy call. They've "been searching for their lost dog." They come to Harrington's house for the dog. The kids use Harrington's shepherd as a decoy. But when Earl and Percy faun all over the dog, pretending it's their long-lost "Rags," the Bike Brigade won't let them take it, saying they have to wait for their parents to come home first. Earl and Percy split.

On their bikes, the brigade follows as Earl and Percy pull away from the curb. From a distance, they follow them as the dognappers check off lost dog ads and pick up dogs. They end up at the lab.

Inside, Earl and Percy unload the dogs. Stan berates them for bringing in a group of small, mangy dogs. Says the lab won't give them as much for those dogs.

Ryan and others try to get into the lab, but they're stopped at the door. Ryan thinks he hears Jupiter bark. The others have to restrain him. The brigade is threatened with a trespassing violation if they don't beat it.

At home, Ryan has his father call the lab, but they deny they have the dog. (Earl on phone next to Jupiter's cage—"Nope, no dog like that here.") And since Jupiter was unlicensed, they can't prove he was their dog anyway. Ryan's father says there's nothing they can do.

But the Bike Brigade decides they can prevent other dogs from being dognapped. The next day, the brigade follows Earl and Percy, preventing them from picking up more dogs. They play havoc with the van: foam, superglue on tires, etc.

At the end of the day, Earl and Percy pull into the parking lot of the local sheriff and the Brigade realizes they can't do this forever. They're going to have to take decisive action. They make a plan. They're going to break into the lab to get Jupiter. But Kyle's got a better idea: His mother is the assistant director of the lab. She's got a key, and he can get it. The Brigade is angry at him—why didn't he tell them before his mom worked at the lab? He hadn't said anything because he didn't want them to think his mother had anything to do with stealing Jupiter, and he knew they'd get mad at him just like they're doing now. He defends his mom—she needs the job, and people are helped by the research. Do they want the key or not?

They sneak out at night—each covering for the other by telling their parents they're at the other's house for the night.

They sneak into the lab, find Jupiter, and let him out. Jupiter and Ryan have a tender reunion, but Harrington gets carried away and lets all the other dogs out, too. Pandemonium. The alarm goes off. They're caught by Earl, Percy, and Stan. It looks bad, but Gail is summoned. She makes Stan let them go. No cops. But since they have no ID, no license, nothing, they can't prove Jupiter is their dog, so they have to leave without him.

At the lab, Jupiter won't stop barking after Ryan, and once Gail has left, Stan tells Earl and Percy to put the dog down as soon as they can sneak him out.

At home, Ryan asks Ned why he didn't get the license for Jupiter like he was supposed to. Ned claims he was going to do it, he just got too busy. It didn't seem that important. Ryan is so angry he runs out of the house, shutting the back door with a slam.

ACT III

Later that night, Ryan hasn't come back home. Ned paces around. He calls Gail. Kyle hasn't seen Ryan either. He calls the others in the Brigade. They don't know where he is, either. He decides to go out looking for him.

Ned finds Ryan sitting out in front of the lab where he can hear Jupiter barking. Ryan's devastated. There's no way to get his dog back. Ned consoles him. He understands about Jupiter. It was Brandon's dog, and that means something to him, too. They both miss Brandon, and there's no way they can bring him back. They shed a tear. Then Ned convinces Ryan he shouldn't abandon a loyal friend just because things have become difficult. Of course, he's still grounded for the break-in, but he should try other means. He'll help in whatever way he can. Ryan tells him about Gail. Okay, that's going to be a little tough. He didn't know she was working at that lab.

The next day, Gail and Ned get into a fight over the dog. Ned doesn't see why she can't free him. She says it can't be Ryan's dog; it's a valuable experimental animal gotten through legitimate channels. Ned tells her to look a little deeper into how they acquired the dog. His son knows his own dog.

Stan, Earl, and Percy deny dog stealing to Gail. They say they get dogs at the pound that would otherwise be euthanized, or they buy them from breeders. Did they steal Jupiter? No, it's a dog they got at the pound. They'd better be telling the truth, or they'll be fired.

Gail phones the pound and inquires about Jupiter. The man at the pound pretends to look through his records, then confirms that Jupiter was indeed retrieved from the pound by Earl and Percy just before the dog was scheduled to be put down.

When the man at the pound hangs up, he immediately calls Earl and Percy and demands that they increase his "finder's fee" an extra $100 this month. When he tells them why, they agree and desperately begin to phony up records to prove where they got Jupiter. Stan tells them the lab is still going to need more dogs. They have a contract. Earl and Percy have to get out there and look for more strays.

Together, Ned and Ryan go to a couple of law firms, but none will take the case without a large retainer. Ned offers to put up the money—even though he doesn't have it—but Ryan stops him. He's given up.

In their backyard, Ryan mopes around. Dad watches concerned from the back window. He makes a phone call. Minutes later, the Bike Brigade swarms the backyard on their bikes. They try to cheer Ryan up, but it's no use. Ryan knew he should never have come to this town. Kyle laments that if they could only prove that Earl and Percy are dognapping . . . That gives Ryan an idea. They can set a trap using Kyle's dog. His mother would recognize that dog, right? If they can get the dognappers in trouble with Gail, they'll get Jupiter back.

On a street where they've seen the van in the past, they leave Kyle's dog tied to a streetlamp and hide. Earl and Percy cruise by, stop, and snatch the dog, while Harrington uses her digital camera to capture the theft. Then they follow Earl and Percy on bikes. Earl and Percy catch on that they're being followed and try to evade. It appears that they give the Brigade the slip . . . But Ryan stops to make a phone call.

Earl and Percy drive around to the back of the lab and pull into the loading dock. Looking both ways, they take the dogs, including Kyle's dog, out of the van. The police and media descend on Earl, Percy, and Stan. The Bike Brigade comes out from cover, along with Ned and Gail, who identifies Kyle's dog. The cops haul off Earl, Percy, and Stan, taking them away in cuffs.

Days later, Dad and Ryan, Kyle and Gail celebrate at a backyard picnic with all the kids and a slew of dogs. Dad plays Frisbee with Ryan and Jupiter, and then we . . .

FADE OUT.

THE END

Lesson Six

PLOT POINT SCENES

What are the most important scenes in a movie? I'd say the opening five minutes and the closing five minutes. In the opening scenes, you learn what kind of a movie it's going to be, the world of the character, and whether you want to be in that world with that person for two hours. You decide in those opening minutes whether you like the movie or not. This is usually confirmed by the closing five minutes, the five minutes you leave with. Those are the ones you refer to later when you're talking about the movie. My daughter loved *Shakespeare in Love* until those closing five minutes, and then she felt cheated because it wasn't, in her eyes, a happy ending. Now she says she hated the film. Lots of people make judgments about film just as easily.

The next most important scenes are the sequences that determine the plot points. There are all kinds of names for these points, but I'll refer to them just as I did in previous lectures: ordinary life, inciting incident, act I curtain (goal and plan), mid- or turning point, act II curtain (low point), final challenge, and return to normal life. Great care should be given to these sequences because they're the backbone of the movie. The major towers in the bridge. And each sequence reflects the overall structure of a movie: There's a bit of ordinary life, an inciting incident, an act I close, a midpoint, a low point, a final challenge, and a return to normal life. Let's look at the plot point scenes in *Thelma & Louise.*

But before we do, let's just take a moment and remember what the most important element of any scene is. Yes, conflict. You already know it. And it will be evident in these scenes, too.

BETTER LATE THAN NEVER

That could be the rallying cry in this movie. It's going to be all about Thelma discovering herself—a little late in her life, but better that than never. It also applies to when the inciting incident comes in. You could say that sequence begins in the country bar they stop at. In a bit of ordinary life, a man, Harlan, tries to pick them up. They talk, and he tells Thelma she should dance with him. In the inciting incident of the sequence, Thelma tells Louise, "You said we was gonna have some fun, so let's have some," and she goes off to dance with the man. That's also her *plan* for this sequence. Act II of the sequence is Thelma and Harlan dancing. She gets a little woozy, and he convinces her to go outside with him. There, he wants to kiss her. This is the midpoint of the sequence, when the action spins off in a different direction. He gets more insistent and hits her, then starts to rape her. That would be the all is lost point of the scene, the end of act II. Louise shows up and puts the gun to his neck in the beginning of act III of the sequence. She gets him off of her, then shoots him. That's the final challenge of the sequence. They escape in the final part of the sequence, which is their return to their normal life—their journey.

Classic construction. The whole thing takes place in less than ten minutes, but we now have a whole new ball game. Their lives are never going to be the same.

Each plot point sequence in the movie follows this type of structure. The end of act I, beginning at around 34:45, starts with them in the car saying they're going to need money. They argue in the hotel room. Louise calls her boyfriend in the inciting incident of the scene. He agrees to help her in the close of act I of the sequence. The midpoint is when she asks him if he loves her—the sequence is going in a different direction now. When he says "Yeah," it's a low point for Louise—the end of act II of the sequence. The act III final challenge is Louise pulling up outside the motel and honking for Thelma. (The decision making is actually the final challenge.) They hit the road again in the return to normal life of this sequence.

If this is confusing, remember to think of each sequence as a mini-movie. It almost always works. Not always, because in creative endeavors there can be no strict rules, but it almost always applies.

The midpoint of the *film* comes with a sequence whose inciting incident happens the night before, when J.D. and Thelma have sex. Her life is never going to be the same again. The second act of the midpoint comes when Thelma enters the restaurant lightheaded after discovering sex. She and Louise talk about it until Louise realizes that Thelma left J.D. alone with the money—this is the midpoint of the midpoint. The whole thing is spun around into a different direction now. They go to the room, and, of course, it's gone. All is lost. The low point of the midpoint sequence. (Are you still with me here?). The third act final challenge of the midpoint consists of Thelma trying to snap Louise out of it. Again, the return to normal is their leaving.

Briefly, the end of act II sequence begins with some ordinary life when they pull into a gas station to fill up. The inciting incident is Thelma calling her husband, and he knows. The midpoint of the close of act II sequence (okay, I hope you've been plotting this on a white board!) is when Slocumb tells them he knows they're going to Mexico. The close of the second act is the close of the act II sequence, when Thelma admits she told J.D. they were going to Mexico and Louise laments that they had two things going for them, and now one of them is gone. The act III final challenge is their realization they're fugitives now, and their decision-making process needs to change: "Let's start behaving like that." And they drive off—again, they return to normal, now changed forever.

The climactic sequence also hits all the traditional points. See if you can plot them.

One thing you have to notice when you look at these scenes is that there is conflict in all of them, even in Louise's conversation with her boyfriend. It's what gives each scene its tension, and it's what keeps a viewer wanting to know more. Look for it in every film you see.

Assignment

1. Revise and expand the second half of your beat sheet to include full descriptions of scenes. With that you will have finished the first draft of your treatment. Again, the Writers Guild also uses the term story for treatment.
2. If you're in a writers group, share the treatments a few days ahead of time so you can give them enough time to settle in your subconscious before you discuss them with the others.

Lesson Seven

LAYERING

Knowing your plot points is first and foremost when developing a story. Understanding who your characters are both helps create those points and flows from them at the same time. Having a good understanding of your character's journey is fundamental. Now you have the skeleton of the movie. But there's more to life than a character's arc. There's more to a movie than one person's struggle.

When you talk to screenwriters in Starbucks, you're likely to hear about "layering." Writers like to pile more meaning, more development, more depth into a script, when left to their own devices. They like to develop subplots, create kooky minor characters, and pay off their setups. So let's talk about enriching your story.

First, let's talk about the most obvious—maintaining conflict in your story. If your character faces a small problem, it's resolved in a scene. If it's larger, then it might take an act to overcome. Larger still, and you've got two acts. Think about how many movies you've seen that felt over in about sixty minutes because that's all it took for the character to resolve their conflict, but you had to sit through thirty minutes of "wrapping up." That was due to either not a big enough problem or not enough resistance to the solution.

Did I just contradict myself? I mean, which is it, not a big enough problem or not enough resistance? You're right, it's both. Let's look at *The Wizard of Oz* for a second. World's easiest problem: Dorothy's goal is simple—she just wants to get home. It's the quality of the opposition to that goal that makes that film. The protagonist must have a worthy opponent, be it a person, place, thing, or even idea.

On the opposite end of the problem scale is Bruce Willis's goal in *Armageddon*. He wants to save the world. Big goal, big movie. One man (with his trusty crew) against the universe. There's really something at stake here.

It doesn't have to be one extreme or the other. There's a whole range in between. The goal must be worthy, the opposition formidable, at least in the character's terms.

Two films come to mind whose characters have similar goals. In *Almost Famous* (written and directed by Cameron Crowe) the aspiring rock journalist just wants to get an interview with the leader of a rock band. That's it. That's his goal. But there are forces working against him. Powerful forces, at least for him—drugs, groupies, egos, endangered airplanes, young love. The conflict, the tension, is maintained by throwing a wall of experience and distraction up against this naïve teenager. It wouldn't truly be worthy of you or me (we like to think), but this boy's about fifteen. It would have been easy to be overcome by the whole heady atmosphere of touring with a rock group. But he fought to maintain his role as a journalist and never forgot what his goal was. Okay, sometimes it wasn't uppermost in his mind, but he usually got back to it. How he grows as he attempts to get the interview is the subject of the movie.

The second film you may not have heard of—*Croupier* (written by Paul Mayersberg, starring a young Clive Owen). A very dark film that breaks a couple of rules while adhering strictly to others, it's the story of a professional gambler whose goal is to write a novel. But he's not a typical professional gambler, he is the "house" side of gambling. He's addicted to the power of the dealer, of watching the suckers lose, of having control over them. His addiction is the reverse of most gamblers', but it stands between him and his goal nonetheless. Until he uses it as the subject matter of his book.

So, the goal must be important, thought it need not be earth shattering. But the obstacles must be difficult, frequent, and varied.

SUBPLOTS AND SUPPORTING PLAYERS

Let's go back to *The Wizard of Oz*, a veritable textbook on screenwriting. Each of the supporting characters is a memorable creation, consistent in both incarnations (on the farm and in Oz). Each has their own arc to follow, their own conflict to overcome. Each supports Dorothy and the main story, but each truly could be extracted to have their own short.

And they, as much as anything else in the movie, make that movie memorable. Yes, we remember Dorothy fondly, but who can forget the Cowardly Lion, the Tin Man, the Scarecrow, or, even, and especially, the Wicked Witch of the West? And she's mean to dogs, too. All these characters (as well as the Great and Terrible Wizard) are set up in the first act as the people in Dorothy's quotidian life. By the end, all achieve either their heart's desire or are vanquished forever, as in the case of the Witch.

Forget about Dorothy. The movie revolving around her is rich enough to remember on its own.

But it is a single piece of fabric. All the subplots tied together have something to do with each other; they're not off in their own movie. If you introduce subplots, and you should, they must have some relation to the rest of the film. Tom Hanks's character in *You've Got Mail* is building a bookstore empire as well as falling in love. In the movie on which Nora Ephron and Delia Ephron based theirs, *The Shop Around the Corner* (screenplay by Samson Raphaelson, based on Miklós László's play), there was a subplot that was a counterpoint to the romance of the main story—the infidelity of the boss's wife with one of the store employees.

In real life there is no central character except you, but no one else seems to recognize that, and they lead their lives as if totally oblivious of the need to support your drama. In a movie they may appear to be oblivious, but supporting characters must have something to do with your central character, either directly or indirectly, either as part of your character's story or as part of a story that somehow illuminates your character.

And again, supporting characters can be the most memorable. Sure, I like *Will & Grace*, but truth be told, they're just ordinary people where I come from. But the supporting players, Jack and Karen . . . now they are a couple of characters. They make the show memorable for me.

How do you create a memorable supporting character? Refer to the second lecture. Or look around your life. How about that barista at the coffeehouse you like to go to? Isn't there something unusual about her? And your mother-in-law—okay, maybe not her, but that friend of hers with the blue hair. And your neighbor who insists on keeping that boat in his driveway, or your roommate from college, the one who slept during the day and played bridge at night (like mine). Combine traits from two or three of these people and you've got something.

The point is, they're going to have a story within the story, something that amplifies what's going on with your central character. Maybe, as in all those 1930s and '40s movies, your romantic leads have sidekicks who will hook up. Or try to prevent your leads from hooking up.

WHAT'S A SETUP?

Simply stated, the setup is a trait, skill, or event that you present early on that has some sort of payoff later. The Wicked Witch appears in Munchkinland and threatens Dorothy. Boy, does that pay off later. "Rosebud," says the dying Citizen Kane. The spine of the movie, it finally pays off when the sled is tossed into the flames (though email me in private for me to tell you, if you don't already know, what it really meant to Hearst). In *Space Cowboys* (screenplay by Ken Kaufman and Howard Klausner), you have the landing simulation scene where Tommy Lee Jones has to bring the shuttle in without the computer. That skill later pays off when Clint Eastwood lands it under similar, "impossible," circumstances. Other skill payoffs: the reconfiguring of the computers, his reconfiguring of the Russian satellite, and so on. That's why they were brought on the mission; they had skills. You've got to make them pay off.

And if you haven't set something up, say that your female lead can ride a rodeo bull, go back and add it in somewhere. Sometimes, you don't know what you're going to need until you get there. Once you get there, do what's necessary, then figure out a place to slot it in early on. It helps the audience understand the character better, follow the story, and not say "Huh? Where'd she learn to do that?"

TIME

There are two kinds of time you have to keep in mind when you construct your story. The first is obvious—you've got between ninety minutes and two hours in which to tell your story. You've got to balance your acts out so that you don't have a fifty-minute first act, a twenty-minute second act, and a twenty-minute third act. It won't be a satisfying movie if it's way out of balance. Mostly, the first act is about thirty minutes (pages), the second is about forty, and the third about twenty-five. Variations abound, but right now don't try to create your own format. Wait until you've got a couple of scripts under your belt before you vary the formula.

So, when you rewrite your treatment, write it with that balance. Play out each scene in your head. How long is it going to take on the screen? As you write, you should be seeing the movie in your head. (And you can cast anybody from any era in it. Ain't the imagination great?) If one or another act is taking too long, look for cuts. Look for cuts anyway. Leave only what moves the story forward.

One thing to remember—eating dinner takes a long time. Walking to the store takes a long time. Sometimes even walking from the car to the house takes a long time. Think about it in terms of your story. Do you want to spend ten minutes (10 percent of your movie) eating breakfast or washing the car? What's going to happen in that time that's worthwhile, that will move the story forward? Usually, you can cut a scene like that altogether or just hint at it happening. Which means no scenes like "they go shopping" or "they play chess." Okay, that last one was uncalled for, but you get the idea.

Then there's the time frame of your story. Does it take place over the course of several generations? Years? Months? Days? Or is it in real time (i.e., does the action really take place in 90–120 minutes)? For your first script, I'd recommend keeping the time frame as short as possible, though a real-time project is hard as hell to do. (I've done one. It's tough.)

It's all about keeping people in their seats for two hours. More than that. Keeping them glued to the *edge* of their seats.

Assignment

1. Revise your treatment. How? Make sure every scene has conflict. Make sure every scene moves the story forward or tells us something new about a main character. Make sure every scene in the movie is there.
2. Make sure all setups pay off.
3. Pinpoint when the central character changes.
4. Discuss the revisions with the others in your group.

Lesson Eight

SUPPORTING CHARACTERS—THE SPICE

Let's talk again about supporting players. If your story has only a protagonist and an antagonist, it's going to be pretty thin. They need friends, colleagues, allies in their battle. And the old adage—you're known by the company you keep—is very true in film. It's one way we learn who the central character is: by the people they surround themself with.

Back to *The Wizard of Oz,* that veritable textbook on screenwriting. Not only do the supporting characters help Dorothy in her quest to return home, but they also represent parts of Dorothy's personality, as Chris Vogler has pointed out in his book, *The Writer's Journey* (highly recommended for writers following the mythic structure, by the way). Or, at least, parts of her personality that need development. The Cowardly Lion helps Dorothy to face things the way they are and not run away from them—a lesson he himself must learn first. The Tin Man underscores Dorothy's need for empathy with others. The Scarecrow, her need to use her wits instead of always relying on her aunt and uncle to get her out of scrapes. Even the Good Witch stands for something inside Dorothy—her innate goodness and love of her home and family. She just needs a little reminding that there's no place like home.

In *The Green Mile,* screenplay by Frank Darabont based on the serial novel by Stephen King, many of the supporting players are there to contrast with Paul as a way of bringing out his character, which, though upright and respectable, is somewhat drab. In the film, there is a rehearsal of an execution in which we see all kinds of behavior and dialogue that sets up Paul and shows him to be a compassionate man despite the fact that he supervises the warehousing and then execution of prisoners. The people around him are compelling in themselves and create interest in the movie for the viewer.

Once the sequence gets underway and Toot begins the rehearsal, we learn just who he is in a pair of lines: "Sittin' down, sittin' down, rehearsing now! Everybody settle!" Toot is comfortable enough with his keeper to feel free to mimic him irreverently. His repetitive speech tells us that he may be missing a few marbles. He makes us laugh in the midst of what should be supremely solemn. And, eventually, he gives Paul the opportunity to point that out, as he does in a later scene when he talks about trying not to laugh in church. So Paul, by contrast, is a compassionate, serious person with respect for human dignity.

In this sequence we also further set up Percy's evil when we see he learns about the wetting of the sponge. Later, his brutal act (not to be confused with the respectable Brutal character) further underlines Paul's innate goodness. We've suspected Percy for some time and have been wondering since the previous scene how his evil is going to manifest itself. Soon we'll know. If Paul is good, Percy is evil.

During the final part of the rehearsal, Paul's compassion and tolerance of Toot is underscored with a roll of his eyes and a choice to ignore the intruding mouse. Contrast this with Percy's behavior in the previous sequence when the mouse outruns him and his traps.

Paul is one determined and compassionate man. How do we know? By how he reacts to the supporting characters, and by how they stand in stark contrast to him.

So, what do your supporting characters support? Are they sounding boards for your central character? Are they contrasts? Or are they really just facets of the central character, as in *The Wizard of Oz*, there to help your character grow and become the person they need to be?

IT'S NOT WRITING, IT'S REWRITING

How many times have you heard someone say, "Scriptwriting isn't writing, it's rewriting?" You haven't? Well, take note here, then, for the first of thousands of times you'll hear it. And it's true. Revisions are a way of life for screenwriters. Revisions according to your own desires, the notes of an executive, the executive's boss, the network, the star, the director, the new director, your mom. Lots of people want to have input. Unless they're paying you directly, listen to their input, but then choose what changes make sense to you, make your story better. If it's not an improvement, don't change it.

When people pay you to make changes, also listen for what makes sense for your story. If it doesn't, try to suggest something else. If they insist, you're going to have to make the change. It's up to you to do the least damage possible to the logic and content of your script. Good luck. It's a struggle for all writers, because we all think that once we say it's done, it's done. And perfect.

But we're wrong. It can always be better. It's hard to go in there and rip your guts out on a continuing basis. But get used to it. Put your ego aside and keep your goal in mind—to make a better script. Whatever serves that goal is good. What doesn't is bad.

And sometimes, notes can really help. Having a fresh perspective can open up new ways of looking at your story, new directions you haven't thought of. Or it just may help stimulate something in you. Suddenly that fix you've been looking for in the third act will come to you, thanks to a well-phrased bit of criticism. I'm sorry, I mean a "note."

So, when making suggestions to your fellow writers, keep that in mind, too. Say things that will improve, in your way of looking at things, their stories. When you listen to a suggestion from another writer, keep in mind they are only interested in improving your work. No personal attacks are meant. We all have the same goal. It doesn't mean you have to agree with every suggestion. It just means you have to sift through it for the truth that might help your work.

Okay, go revise your stories (treatments). Again. By next week, you should have a blueprint for a movie.

Assignment

1. Polish your treatment. Are the supporting characters well developed? Do they help define the central character? Discuss with your writers group.
2. Incorporate any feedback you may have received, but only if it improves the story you are telling.
3. What does *polish* mean? It doesn't mean to rewrite the whole thing. It means make minor adjustments to the story, if necessary. It means making sure every sentence makes sense and needs to be there. It means checking for grammar, spelling, and punctuation.

Lesson Nine

DIALOGUE—THE NEXT FRONTIER

It should be easy to write good dialogue. We all talk, right? Some of us are even great conversationalists. If our own imagination fails us, we can rely on the speech of friends and acquaintances, even strangers if we're discreet. That's what audio recorders are for, right? There's only one problem—it wouldn't be the dialogue of *your* characters in *your* scene moving toward *your* conclusions.

But there is a lot to learn by listening carefully to conversations. You'll hear the starts and stops people make. The repetitions. The elliptical nature of many conversations. The "off-subject" talk that's really on subject. The humor that sometimes sneaks into everyday speech. The "uhs" and "you knows" and stuttering. Making your characters sound natural can be quite a job. Making them distinct from one another even more of a task.

One of the first things that tells you about a character is what that character sounds like. Their level of education, their place of origin, their state of mind—all are reflected in their speech. Think of *Forrest Gump.* Think of *Coal Miner's Daughter.* Captain Kirk in *Star Trek* sounds different from Spock, who sounds very different from

Spike Lee in *She's Gotta Have It,* and Easy Rawlins in *Devil in a Blue Dress,* and Jimmy Smits in *Mi Familia,* and Nakia in *Black Panther: Wakanda Forever.*

So there are two questions I should answer here: What is good dialogue, and how do you get it? Let me answer the first in a facile way and hope I can point you to answers for the second.

Good dialogue is dialogue that sounds natural, that sounds particular to your character, and that works in your scene and in the genre of your film. (Thank you for stating the obvious, Paul.) Maybe it would be more instructive to state what *bad* dialogue is. Okay, how about Shakespearean English in a hip-hop film? How about long speeches in an action picture? Intellectual dialogue in a love scene?

Okay, again with the obvious. But I swear I've read them all (or heard them).

Let's have a look at some good dialogue that moves a scene forward, that tells us about our characters, and that sounds real.

Watch *Get Shorty* (screenplay by Scott Frank based on the novel by Elmore Leonard) right now. Or, better yet, read the book.

As a matter of fact, read anything by Elmore Leonard, the master of dialogue. Frank was smart enough to copy his style, if not his exact words, in the screenplay.

Okay, cue up the film to the scene where Harry, the film producer, goes downstairs to investigate some voices in Karen's study. He listens at the door, hears Letterman on the tube. Doesn't see anyone in the dark room. When he enters, the TV screen goes black and the desk lamp comes on.

We've already met Chili Palmer by now, so we've heard him speak. Not necessarily grammatical, but clean and sparse. To the point. He's got a goal, but he doesn't state it immediately. He's in total control of the situation, despite the conflict that comes up between them in the first line of the scene. "Jesus Christ," Harry says, shocked that someone's broken into the house. And we're off on an interesting conversation that ultimately leads to very unexpected places. And they're in conflict throughout the scene.

THE SHORTEST DISTANCE

It's all direct and to the point. Sometimes the best dialogue is indirect. Sometimes it appears to be about one thing when it really is about another. Let's look at *The Godfather Part II* (screenplay by Francis Ford Coppola and Mario Puzo, based on Mario Puzo's novel) for an example. Do you recall the scene (and if you don't, or you've never seen the first two Godfather films, go watch them now. I mean it.) where the Robert Duvall character, the consigliere, is talking to Pentangeli, the mobster who has turned state's evidence against the Corleone family? They're walking and talking about the Roman empire and what would happen to loyal Romans who made a single, ill-advised mistake. How they might fall on their sword to avoid embarrassment and keep the natural order of things. The entire conversation, some of which deals in specifics about what would happen to such a person's family, is a bargaining process between them. They discuss what's happening and what each will be expected to do in the future. No specific agreement is reached—on the surface. But they come to an agreement nonetheless, in Roman terms.

On another side of the subtext coin is the type of conversation you're more likely to have heard in real life. Usually, it has to do with sex. Have kids? Ever talk about sex in front of them without using explicit language? Sure you have. Called the act by another name? Gettin' some "sugar"? (Okay, whatever name you use for it.) Then here's another film you have to watch just to listen to the dialogue between Bogart and Bacall—*The Big Sleep* (screenplay by William Faulkner (!) based on the book by Raymond Chandler). In it, the Bogart character, Philip Marlowe, is talking with the Lauren Bacall character over drinks. Ostensibly the conversation is about horse racing and saddles, but they're really describing the kind of sexual partners and experiences they're seeking.

If you can have characters say one thing and let your audience see through it to another, like Faulkner did in this movie, then you've created some interesting dialogue.

Have a look at *The Fall Guy.* The central characters, played by Ryan Gosling and Emily Blunt, often talk about their relationship as the subtext while discussing the movie within a movie that they are making. It's clear to us, and even to the crew, who they're really talking about, but it's more interesting this way.

But dialogue has limitations, no matter how good it is. Action is quicker. They're called *motion* pictures, and if you can move your story forward with moving pictures only, you'll make more of an impression on your audience than if you rely entirely on dialogue. If you illuminate your character through a physical attribute or something he does, it's always going to be better than having you tell about it in dialogue.

Show it, don't tell it.

DIALOGUE TO AVOID

Avoid soliloquies. They're okay in plays, but they stop the action cold in a movie. Avoid any character talking to himself for any reason unless you make that a specific, conscious trait that others know about, because people rarely talk out loud to themselves except for an occasional expletive. Avoid telling jokes unless there's a point to them. Avoid telling one character about something that's already happened in the movie, as your reader or viewer already has the information. Avoid exposition. Or use exposition as ammunition. In other words, bring out the facts you want the audience to know by having a conversation with a lot of conflict.

The best exposition is shown in action, not told in dialogue.

Assignment

1. Print out your treatment. Put it in a drawer and let it sit for two weeks.
2. Start thinking about how your characters sound. Review your character sketches to remind yourself of their backgrounds, ages, education, and status.
3. Reward yourself in whatever way you do for finishing a treatment for a screenplay. It's not easy. You deserve a reward.
4. You might go to a movie with your writers group and discuss it afterward. Was the central character well set up? Did they face significant challenges? Was the structure effective? How would you have improved the story?

Lesson Ten

THE BUSINESS OF WRITING

Show business is both a business and an art. I've been talking about the art and how to make it. But it's a tough business, too, and you have to approach it as such. Here are my thoughts on how to do that.

1. I have enough competition. So why don't you get off the net and study to be real estate agents?
2. If you must write, decide what kind of writing you want to do, i.e., film or episodic television. Have a polished script ready. Have another one. Rewrite them. Rewrite them again. Rewrite them seven or eight times. Register your scripts at the Writers Guild at 3rd and Fairfax in Los Angeles or online at https://www.wgawregistry.org/regfaqs.aspx.
3. Try to get referrals from someone you know. Try to hand your script to someone who can recommend you to someone (not me) who can recommend you to an agent or a producer. Try every relative you have. Ask all your friends.
4. Get the list of franchised agents from the WGA at 3rd and Fairfax or online.

5. Call the agent, don't write to them. If referred, be sure to tell the gatekeeper (possibly the agent's assistant) who referred you. Be friendly to the gatekeeper. Tell them the truth. Ask for help.
6. Call another agent. And another one.
7. Interview the agent who is interested in your work. What would be the agent's plan to get your work read? How many clients do they have? Are you going to be a big fish in a small pond or a small fish in a big pond? Decide if you want to go with an agency that has clout, or if you want to go with a specific agent for some reason. (You might "vibe" with that agent, for example.)
8. Go with the agent who you feel the most connection to and who has the most enthusiasm for your work. If you don't have a choice, sign up with one anyway; you can start moving on from there—it's easier to find an agent once you have one.
9. Read trade weeklies and online publications such as *The Hollywood Reporter* or *Deadline*. Go to as many guild or academy (TV or motion picture) screenings, receptions, and special presentations as you can get into. Network.
10. Once you get in, suck up to whomever you can. I'm serious. Listen more than talk, especially in a writers room on a television show. Don't be smarter than the person in charge. Or the one down from them. Or the one down from that. You're on the bottom.
11. Be persistent. In the end, it isn't going to be raw talent that gets you the job: There are lots of talented people out there. It's going to be persistence. You can do that.

Course 2

SCREENWRITING II: WORKS IN PROGRESS

Much of the content of the second course lectures in the series repeats material from the first course since many of the students were new to my method. In the following pages, I will present only new material, some of which is taken from other online courses I taught. If you need to refresh yourself on screenwriting terms and process, check out the glossary and reread sections from Introduction to Screenwriting I as you need.

Lesson One

TIME TO TWEAK

I know you've already written a treatment—sometimes called an outline (inaccurately) or a story—in your previous course. But I make no assumption as to its suitability for conversion into a screenplay. It may be fully beaten out, its premise and characters clear, its acts neatly defined, its story gripping. If that's the case, and there is nothing you can do to improve it, just go up to the stage now and collect your Oscar because you belong to a minute group of geniuses, the hems of whose robes I'd love to touch.

Everyone's treatment needs just one more tweak, one more set of eyes on it, one more pass to bring it up to another level. As a matter of fact, some writers believe this so fervently that they can never finish their stories, and thus never actually begin their screenplays (or never reach a "final" draft of their screenplay in a variation of this condition). You're not going to have that problem, however. Yes, with the information you glean from this course, you're going to polish your story, but you will also get into the screenplay itself, completing at least 50 percent of it if you keep up. And I'm confident you'll be able to do that. I taught an in-person class in UCLA's School of Theater, Film, and Television's Professional Screenwriting Program and in their MFA program where we went from premise to fade out in ten weeks. It's a slog, but it can be done. (I've done it in one week, but there were chains and industrial quantities of caffeine involved.)

But before we write `FADE IN` at the top of the page, let's do a little review and a lot of thinking. The better your story, the better (and easier to write) will be your screenplay. (Though it's never really easy. Don't kid yourself.)

Assignment

Some of these are the same assignments you should have done previously, but it wouldn't hurt to review them to see if they are still in keeping with your treatment.

1. Reread the first chapter of *The Art of Dramatic Writing* by Lajos Egri, where he introduces the concept of premise.
2. Read the first ten pages or watch the first ten minutes of *Tin Cup* and *His Girl Friday*. You can find printed versions of the scripts in *Scenario* magazine, volume I, No. 4 (*His Girl Friday*) and *Scenario* magazine, volume II, No. 4 (*Tin Cup*). Please note that these are not strictly in screenplay format because of space constraints. You should be able to rent the videos and find the scripts on most online script sites. Doing both is recommended.
3. If necessary, revise treatments with character and structure in mind.
4. Buy *The Screenwriter's Bible, 7th Edition: A Complete Guide to Writing, Formatting, and Selling Your Script*, by David Trottier. Use this as a guide to formatting your screenplay (also see an example of formatting on page 105).
5. If you're in a writers group and discussing your treatments, discuss what needs to be changed in your treatment or what can be left to revise in the script itself.
6. Write socko first five pages of screenplay. Go over them again. Did you introduce the main character? Does each line belong? Is there at least one memorable line of dialogue that could be quoted in the ad?

Screenplay Format Sample

Here's how the first five pages might look.

```
                                    FADE IN:

INT. DENTIST'S OPERATORY - DAY

AVERY GOLD, a young-looking 60s, is deep into
the mouth of a patient, PAUL, who is wearing
a rubber dental dam. Avery drills and sings
along with a rock song from the '70s that
plays on the office sound system.

He never looks the patient nor the assistant,
CONNIE, in the eye.

                    AVERY
              (singing along)
      You hear me. I hear you. You want
      me. I need you. Ohohoh, baby,
      your body is talking. My body is
      listening. We're gonna--

                    CONNIE
      --It's in the rotation again.

                    AVERY
      Ka-ching! Another two and a half
      cents into the retirement fund.

                    PAUL
      Uh. Ugh. Uh. Unk?

                    AVERY
      Please don't try to talk, Paul.
      One little bump and that molar's
      history.
```

PAUL
Un. Unk. Unk?

AVERY
No, I never recorded it myself. Wrote it, though.

PAUL
Uh-huh?

AVERY
Hold still, please! The dam is in there for a reason.
(to CONNIE)
More suction.

The patient squirms.

PAUL
Un unk?

AVERY
Yes, I wrote a few songs for them before there was a them.

PAUL
Um. Ung?

AVERY
They're called Sudden Deth. Now, will you hold still before this turns into a root canal?

PAUL
Un Ung. Unh-unh?

AVERY
You never heard of Sudden Deth? They were bigger than Humble Pie.

PAUL
Un unh.

AVERY
J. Geils Band?

PAUL
Un unh.

AVERY
Never mind. Ancient history. Let's focus here.
(to CONNIE)
Can you mix up some gunk? We have a big one here.

PAUL
Ung?

AVERY
It's the technical term. Oh shit!

PAUL
(agitated)
Ung!

AVERY
Just kidding. Everything's all right.
(to CONNIE)
Connie, could you look up molar in the manual?

PAUL
(more agitated)
Unh unh!

AVERY
Gotcha!

EXT. LOUIE'S SMART MART - EVENING

Avery pulls up in his late model Acura. Parks in front of this modest convenience store. Gets out of the car and enters the store.

INT. LOUIE'S SMART MART - CONTINUOUS

Avery enters. At the register ...

LOUIE

Also 60s, bald but long hair on the sides pulled into a gray ponytail, waves.

LOUIE
Avery!

AVERY
Louie. What's new?

LOUIE
New York, New Jersey.

AVERY
Numismatic. Come on. Get some new material.

LOUIE
I will if you promise to buy something new like a pastrami sandwich or something.

AVERY
What's the matter, out of roast chicken?

Louie reaches behind the counter, pulls out a roast chicken sandwich.

LOUIE
Naw. Saved one for you, but, come

```
      on, Avery ... How about a bottle of
      IPA instead of Heineken?

                    AVERY
      Never toured the IPA factory. Just
      wrap it up, willya?

As Louie bags the sandwich and the beer ...

                    LOUIE
      Guess who's coming to town?

                    AVERY
      Santa Claus?

                    LOUIE
      Better. Sudden Deth. And Russ's
      fronting them again.

                    AVERY
      Thanks for the sandwich and the
      beer.

                    LOUIE
      What, you don't care?

                    AVERY
      He's someone else's root canal now.

                    LOUIE
      I hear The James is gonna be here
      for the concert.

                    AVERY
      He's out?

                    LOUIE
      Got out last week. I give him six
      months this time.
```

AVERY
They don't call him the Folsom Boomerang for nothing.

LOUIE
We could all hang out after the show.

AVERY
Yeah, great. Except for one thing.

LOUIE
Yeah, I know. The apology.

AVERY
The apology.

Avery hands Louie some cash. Louie waves it away.

LOUIE
Every fifth sandwich is free.

AVERY
Thanks. Same for every fifth crown.

LOUIE
I'm close ...

INT./EXT. AVERY'S ACURA - EVENING

As Avery enters the car, starts it up, backs out ... listens ... the NPR station. Someone's droning on ...

NPR VOICE (V.O.)
... in the remote villages near the source of the Rio Plata, men and women--

Avery jabs at the buttons on the radio.

NEWS VOICE (V.O.)
--the president announced this morning--

Avery jabs at the buttons again.

This time an unrecognizable rock band comes on. Avery's head starts bobbing to the music ...

DISSOLVE TO:

Lesson Two

SCREENWRITERS READ

One of the best ways to become educated as to form and structure, pacing and just plain storytelling, is to read filmscripts. Do a search for screenplays on the net and you'll find hundreds of places to buy screenplays or read them for free. Most big bookstore chains have 'em, as does Amazon (they even sell some teleplays I wrote for *The Twilight Zone* with my former screenwriting partner, Jeremy Finch).

Many college libraries now have screenplay collections, or they at least have old copies of *Scenario*, which has four screenplays in each issue, though not in screenplay format. Read as many screenplays as you can.

If you live in the Los Angeles area, try the libraries listed below. You can't generally take screenplays out, but they only take about an hour or two to read. And you can play the movie in your head the way the writer meant it to be.

Did I mention that you should read as many screenplays as you can? You should.

SOME SCRIPT RESOURCES

AMPAS MARGARET HERRICK LIBRARY

333 S. La Cienaga Blvd.
Beverly Hills, CA 90211

Scripts available online and in person, though not all scripts have been digitized.

AFI LOUIS B. MAYER LIBRARY

2021 N. Western Ave.
Los Angeles, CA 90027

On-site use of scripts by fellows, faculty, alumni, and staff, plus researchers by appointment only.

WRITERS GUILD FOUNDATION SHAVELSON-WEBB LIBRARY

7000 W. 3rd St.
Los Angeles, CA 90048

On-site use of scripts (icluding TV scripts) by appointment only. No copying allowed.

ONLINE

There are many sites offering free or low-cost screenplays popping up every day. Here are two that have been helpful to me:

Simply Scripts (www.simplyscripts.com)
Drew's Script-o-Rama (www.script-o-rama.com)

PHONE CONVERSATIONS

You'll find several ways to write phone conversations in the scripts you'll read. Phone conversations and texting are common occurrences in daily life. As such, they're hard to avoid when writing a film that takes place in the twenty-first century. Still, avoid them whenever possible by using direct, in person, dialogue, which is more dynamic, visual, and easier to understand. But if you must use a phone conversation, here are a couple of ways to write one.

INT. PAUL'S OFFICE - DAY

Paul bangs away at his keyboard trying to express his anguish. He stops, picks up the handset of his landline phone, and punches in a number.

PAUL
(into phone)
Hi, Wendy. It's Paul for Barbara.

Paul taps his fingers to an imaginary rhythm. Then ...

INTERCUT WITH:

INT. HIS AGENT'S OFFICE - DAY

BARBARA, well preserved, reads a paperback book called REWRITE.

ASSISTANT (O.S.)
Barbara, it's Paul on line 2.

BARBARA
I can't believe he called me. He never calls me.

She grabs the phone.

BARBARA
(into phone)
Hey, Paul.

PAUL
Hi, Barbara.

BARBARA
Paul! I was just reading your book. Great ideas here. I want all my writers to get a copy.

PAUL
Done. But I'm really calling about that lunch you were supposed to set up with Larry David.

It's up to the director to cut back and forth at their discretion. Here's another way to write it, strictly focusing on Paul.

```
INT. PAUL'S OFFICE - DAY

Paul bangs away at his keyboard trying to express
his anguish. He stops, picks up the handset of his
landline phone, and punches in a number.

                    PAUL
              (into phone)
     Hi, Wendy. It's Paul for Barbara.

Paul taps his fingers to an imaginary rhythm.
Then ...

                    BARBARA (V.O.)
     Hey, Paul.

                    PAUL
     Hi, Barbara.

                    BARBARA (V.O.)
     Paul! I was just reading your book.
     Great ideas here. I want all my writers
     to get a copy.

                    PAUL
     Done. But I'm really calling about
     that lunch you were supposed to set
     up with Larry David.
```

There's another way, which would be split screen. Just start it the same way, but instead of writing in INTERCUT WITH, write SPLIT SCREEN and let the director and editor work it out.

Assignment

1. Read over the opening five pages of your screenplay. Is there something to hook the reader before the end of the first page? Do we see the central character's flaw? Do we understand their world and why change is necessary? Do we like your protagonist, or are we at least fascinated by them? Before going on to the next five pages, revise the first five to make them sing.
2. Write the next five pages. Show us the ordinary, day-to-day life of your protagonist.
3. If you are in a writers group, it would be good to read at least five pages of each script out loud. Assign parts, including someone to read the directions (the action). Before you listen to the dialogue, ask yourself and your colleagues these questions: Does the dialogue sound real? Do the characters all sound the same, or are they differentiated? Is there information in the dialogue that could have been better presented in action?

Lesson Three

CONFLICT AND THE SCENE

Just in case I haven't mentioned it sufficiently, let me underline it again: **The element most new (and many experienced) screenwriters leave out of their scenes is conflict.** Without conflict, there is no drama. Without drama (even in a comedy), there is no story. Without conflict, there is no movement. No change. Conflict is the key element of each scene.

The central characteristic, the one element that every scene needs, is conflict.

There, I've said it again.

Just as there are barriers (conflict) for the protagonist to overcome over the length of the film, so, too, there are smaller conflicts in each scene. In the beginning of a scene, somebody wants something. Somebody else either tries to prevent them from getting it or wants something in opposition. The scene, then, is about the struggle. Learning what each character wants is the beginning of the scene. The struggle to get it is the middle. One or the other character wins the struggle. That's the end of the scene. Somebody's got to win, somebody's got to lose.

Every major player in a scene has an objective—they want something. Usually, each character wants something different. Hence the conflict. We must also know what the emotion of that character is at the beginning of the scene, what their attitude is, what their long-term goal is.

There's a helluva difference between a scene that starts off with everyone pissed off at each other from the get-go and one that starts with laughter. If you know your characters, you'll know what their emotions are at the beginning of the scene—are they happy, sad, angry?—and what will happen to them during the scene. Unless they have cause to change (they may or may not), they should maintain that emotion throughout the scene. Actors look at scenes this way (or the good ones do), and they look for hints the writer has given them.

We also need to know what the subject and purpose of the scene is. Yes, it's to move the story forward, first and foremost. But it may also be to shed some light on a character, to reveal information, to provide an obstacle. Know what you want to get across with your scene.

Assignment

1. Read over the last five pages you wrote. Is there conflict in every scene? Make changes if necessary.
2. Write five more pages of your screenplay, focusing on conflict. You should be nearing the inciting incident. While there's no law that says it must happen by a certain page, generally it takes place between pages thirteen and eighteen, with page fifteen a good place to put it. If, however, you have a good reason to put it early, do that. If you need to develop your protagonist more, you can put it later. Just make sure it's not so late that your audience (reader) is tapping their fingers in exasperation. Or not so early that your audience doesn't yet care about what happens to your central character.
3. If you're in a writers group, read another five pages out loud. Is the dialogue easy to say? Does it sound natural? Or are the readers having trouble with your words? What can you do to make the dialogue leap off the page?

Lesson Four

MORE ON DIALOGUE

Locale can affect dialogue. The atmosphere of a place can lend and demand status. Think about architecture. What buildings and surroundings are designed to make you feel small, as if you're in the presence of something bigger than you? What about Saint Peter's Basilica, the Capitol Building in Washington, the office of the CEO of a large company?

And what are some other buildings or objects, designed to make you feel bigger, important, significant? Houses, cafés, buses, cars?

Surroundings and situations also manipulate status. Any human community does it—the UN, the music industry, a group of friends in a bar. One of the things that makes a community is the intent to define status and the role of status. This decision is collective and based on the values and necessities of the group. A man talking about the smell of a rose can be appreciated by a garden club, but they'll laugh at him in the local bar. A person who blows himself up is a terrorist to one group and a martyr to another.

Status is very fluid. Imagine a chief of state talking to an audience. They have the highest status, right? But what happens if a delegate has a heart attack? Now, a doctor comes forward. They have the highest status because everyone is waiting for them to take charge of the situation. So the status has changed because the circumstances of the room have changed.

This happens in conversations. One person knows nothing about sports, so when the conversation is *about* sports, that person has low status. But let's say they're an engineer. Then, when talking about how to build a space station, they will have much higher status in a group of normal people.

So, from place to place, community to community, moment to moment, we are always fighting for status on a playing field that is constantly changing.

Watch the scene near the middle in *Shakespeare in Love* in which Wessex tells Viola that her father has bought him for her, and they are to be married. How many times does status change between them?

Assignment

1. Write a dialogue between two people. Assign each person a status—very low, low, high, or very high. In the first part of the dialogue, each person must maintain the status they started the scene with. In the middle, find a way to change each one to a new status and maintain it for the rest of the conversation. Refer to the scene in *Shakespeare in Love* if you're not sure how status changes affect the tone of a conversation.
2. Read over the last five pages you wrote in your screenplay. Make changes if necessary.
3. Write five more pages of your screenplay. Your inciting incident scene or sequence should be started by now. Is it important enough to compel your protagonist to have to make a life change?
4. In your writers group, discuss the status of each person in your latest pages.

Lesson Five

AN AMERICAN CLASSIC

Is there a classic American film that has more memorable lines in it than *The Wizard of Oz*? From "We're off to see the Wizard" to "Lions and tigers and bears, oh my," the words of Noel Langely, Florence Ryserson, and Edgar Allan Woolf have entered the culture. Their characters, too, based on L. Frank Baum's books, have taken their place in the pantheon of American icons. What makes this film one of the most beloved in American cinema? Courage.

No, wait, that's what the Cowardly Lion would have said. *Structure* is the correct answer.

Yes, there's lots more to it, but the vibrant characters, the fantasy world, the black-and-white and color segments, the songs and dances, all hang on a nearly textbook perfect structure that enables it all to happen. If you haven't seen this film in the last ten days, watch it before you read any further. Thanks.

Okay, welcome back. The modern screenplay relies on the three-act structure that's been tested for over 2,500 years and proven safe. Maybe you've read about it in more detail in Syd Field's *Screenplay* or in Blake Snyder's *Save the Cat!*, but for the moment, let's just talk the basics. Just as a solid framework is necessary for the construction of a good building, a sound three-act format is fundamental for screenplay construction. Yes, it can be done in other ways, but the majority of films employ this basic blueprint for success.

REVIEW OF THE BASICS OF STRUCTURE

The first act of a screenplay is the setup, the second is the conflict, the third is the resolution.

More specifically, the opening ten to fifteen minutes usually show the hero in their normal life. It's when we get to learn who they are. To know them is to care about them. Then something out of the ordinary happens that changes their life and forces them to take some sort of action, though they may not know what that action is for another fifteen minutes or so. At the end of the first act, it's clear what the hero must do to achieve some sort of goal, be it finding the treasure, winning the race, or getting the girl. They have a plan.

Act II is when the hero faces the challenges along the way, the obstacles that fate (and the writer) have thrown between them and the goal. In the middle of act II, there is often a midpoint when the action spins off in an unexpected direction. More obstacles follow that lead the hero to a point of despair when all seems lost, a low point, at the end of act II.

Act III is about the character pulling themself together and making a huge effort to overcome the barriers that stand in their way. Often, the goal has changed by this point. Usually, except in some action and comedy films, the hero has undergone a transformation in themself, having overcome something inside that had prevented them from reaching their goal. The end of the act is the resolution. Either the hero finds the treasure or learns something more valuable than the treasure. Gets the girl or loses her but is a better person for the journey. The original goal, or its substitute, is achieved. The hero is transformed by the journey, and so are we (in the best films). All this usually in service of a premise or a theme.

How does *The Wizard of Oz* fit this paradigm? There's no place like home. You should look in your own backyard for your heart's desire. That's the theme stated by Dorothy when Glinda, the Good Witch of the North, asks her what she's learned. You *can* go back home. And you should. So how does the movie start? With Dorothy running home after her encounter with Miss Gulch, a real witch of a woman (though we only know her through Dorothy's telling of the experience at this stage). Dorothy tries to explain what happened to a very busy Auntie Em but doesn't find a sympathetic ear until she gets to the farmhands. Yet her problem is clear—she needs to protect Toto from Miss Gulch.

Now the foreshadowing starts. Each of the farmhands is going to turn up later. Each exhibits a trait that will identify him when he reappears in Dorothy's dreamworld. Hunk, who later turns up as the Scarecrow, makes several references to "using your head." He goes so far as to accuse Dorothy of not having any brains. "I have so got brains," she says. "Then why don't you use them? Your head ain't made of straw, you know."

Of course, later in the film, brains are what the Scarecrow desperately wants, though whenever real thinking is necessary, he's the one who does it. Each of the farmhands represents a trait that Dorothy herself needs to develop, and will, with the help of the Tin Man, the Scarecrow, and the Lion.

Zeke, who feeds the pigs, counsels her about Gulch: "She ain't nothing to be afraid of. Have a little courage." Zeke turns out to be afraid of pigs when Dorothy falls into the sty. But, importantly, he puts that fear aside to save her. His later incarnation is as the Cowardly Lion. We'll see later how he, too, puts aside his fear in order to rescue Dorothy.

Hickory is the least developed farmhand because, frankly, it's hard to show someone as heartless. But he does pose in a Tin Man posture.

So, each trait is already found in its corresponding character. Each trait would be ideal for Dorothy, and the audience, to have.

So far, we've just met some of the characters, but Dorothy hasn't found much to help her solve her problem. She dreams of "somewhere over the rainbow" where she can't get into any trouble. Somewhere other than where she is.

Moments later, Gulch is introduced riding her bike (not quite a broomstick, but it works). Dorothy even calls her a wicked old witch, and with good reason. She's come to take Toto to be destroyed. Dorothy is beside herself, but when Toto escapes, she decides to run away. This is the inciting incident, the event that propels the movie, that changes Dorothy's life. Her goal now is to find "Somewhere over the rainbow" where she and Toto can live without fear. She runs away.

The first person she meets on her journey is the Professor, who has "magical" powers. He will later turn up as the gatekeeper at Oz and as the Wizard himself, but for now, he looks into the crystal ball and tells Dorothy things that make her want to return home. Her goal is now reset. But a tornado intervenes, and she's locked out of the storm cellar. She's knocked out in her house, and when she wakes up, she's in Munchkinland. She's landed "over the rainbow." And she's a hero with the locals for killing the witch (such wish fulfillment!). But now her goal has become more difficult: She must get out of Oz to be able to return home. The antagonist makes another appearance, this time as the Wicked Witch of the West—the same actor as Miss Gulch, now in green makeup and black robes. Dorothy learns that the ruby slippers have power, though she doesn't know how to use that power. But she desperately wants to return home. Now that her goal has been restated, she gets a plan from Glinda—she's got to go to Oz to see the Wizard. That's the end of act I.

Act II begins when Dorothy sets out on her journey to Oz, following the yellow brick road. Now, in classic fashion, she gathers her team—the characters who will help her achieve her goal. Each of these team members also has a goal: The Scarecrow feels he's a "failure because he hasn't got a brain." Dorothy figures that the Wizard might be able to give him a brain, though we see that he's already quite clever when he tricks the apple trees into throwing them their fruit. Next, she discovers the Tin Man, who is standing frozen in the same pose that Hickory had taken on the Gale farm. He wastes no time before telling them he doesn't have a heart.

Then the Wicked Witch of the West reappears, threatening Dorothy and her team, who now swear they'll help her whether or not they achieve their own goals. Before long, the Lion surprises them in the forest, but he crumbles into tears when Dorothy slaps him. He admits to being a coward, much the same way Zeke had to admit he was afraid of the pigs he tended.

With her team completely assembled, much the way teams in hundreds of films from the *The Magnificent Seven* to *Armageddon* have been assembled, Dorothy sets out for Oz, only to be temporarily stymied by the poppies the Witch has put in her path. She doesn't overcome this on her own, but with Glinda's help. Then Dorothy and her gang reach Emerald City—the midpoint of the film, when things begin to go in a new direction.

Dorothy must deal with more obstacles here: the gatekeeper is reluctant to let her in; the Wizard sends her to find the Witch's broomstick; and the flying monkeys capture her. This would be the low point in Dorothy's journey. All appears lost. It's the end of act II.

Now there's a ticking clock for the action. The Witch has set an hourglass. The red sand of the hourglass trickles down like drops of blood, just as Dorothy's life trickles away. But Toto escapes. Toto, who brought this whole thing about in the first place when he attacked Miss Gulch, goes to get Dorothy's team. And the team responds gladly. The Cowardly Lion is not so cowardly when it comes to saving Dorothy, just as he was as Zeke when he pulled her from the sty.

To achieve entry into the castle, each of the characters uses his own talent—the Tin Man uses his axe, the Scarecrow his brain, and the Lion his courage. They succeed in reaching Dorothy, and she, importantly, succeeds in destroying the witch herself. Now they return to the Wizard so they may return home.

The Wizard turns out to be a fake, of course, but he still promises to help. Once again, Toto escapes, and Dorothy is stranded in Oz. But then Glinda returns and tells her the specific powers of the ruby slippers.

Now that Dorothy has learned that there's no place like home, she has the power to return there. And she does. The resolution.

In the remaining scene, Dorothy wakes up, wraps up the story (with all the characters revisiting her), and we're out.

Setup. Inciting incident. Development of goal. Decision to take action. Act I curtain. Implementing the plan. Challenges. Midpoint. More challenges. Act II curtain (low point). Act III—final push. Resolution. Return to normal life.

Hundreds of movies are made every year using this simple structure. Of course, there's lots more texture to this movie—its characters, its music, its costumes and sets. But it all hangs on the structure.

As you watch movies this week, see where these elements occur in the films. Far from spoiling your movie experience, this understanding of basic structure will enhance it, giving you a deeper appreciation of the screenwriter's craft.

Assignment

1. Read over the last five pages you wrote in your screenplay. Make changes if necessary.
2. Write five more pages. Is your character moving toward a decision? Are things getting more difficult for them? Are the consequences of their action or inaction becoming clear?
3. Watch your favorite movie again with a stopwatch or a clock. Can you find the major plot points in it? Where do they come in terms of time? Are your script's points where they need to be for your story (not necessarily at the same points as your favorite movie)?
4. In your writers group, talk about where and when you write. Do you have a set time each day? Do you have a quiet place, or do you like to write at a local café? Maybe experiment this week with another writer's choices.

Lesson Six

THE CENTRAL EMOTIONAL RELATIONSHIP

We go to watch movies because of the people *in* the movies. Even movies loaded with special effects must have people in them, people about whom we care. And it's not just about the people, it's about the people relating to other people. To be more precise, it's about your central character relating to another person.

In every movie, even action movies, there must be a central emotional relationship. This is one way to humanize your protagonist. It's a way to show their emotional journey as well as their "story" journey (the one focused on their primary goal). It's a way to relate to the protagonist on a human level and to root for them. It's a way to ground the story in an emotional reality that everyone can understand.

It doesn't have to be a romantic relationship. It can be a buddy relationship, as in *Thelma & Louise*. It can be a stand-in father/daughter relationship, as in *Million Dollar Baby*. It can be a mentor/student relationship, as in *Star Wars*. The point is, there must be an emotional relationship at the core of your movie to give it heart.

There are two forms this emotional relationship can take. Either it is an emotional relationship that must be established or one that must be repaired. Sometimes, this relationship is the center of the movie, as in romantic comedies like *The Philadelphia Story*. Sometimes the relationship is the "B" story and serves to support the "A" story, as in *Armageddon*.

Does your story have a key emotional relationship? If it doesn't, now's the time to create one or beef one up. And the emotional relationship should, like your movie, have a beginning, a middle, and an end. As a matter of fact, it should follow the same seven-point paradigm that your "A" story follows. Often, the story points for your emotional story correspond to the "A" story points, but not always. They'll be close, though.

This is the emotional heart of the picture, and even a rough-and-tumble picture like *Die Hard* has one. As a matter of fact, that's what makes the picture so memorable—it has a heart. In every movie there is a relationship to be established or repaired. That's the "B" story.

Actually, in a romance or romantic comedy, the typical "A" story becomes the "B" story and the emotional "B" story becomes the "A" story. Let's have a look at two very different movies, *Die Hard* and *Life as We Know It*.

In *Die Hard*, there's no doubt that the "A" story is about the takeover of the skyscraper by a terrorist group, though the movie starts out as a relationship pic—Willis's John McClane is going out to Los Angeles to see if he can win his family back or at least pay them a civil visit. Soon, the terrorists take over the building his wife works in and hold her and the other workers hostage. McClane's goal becomes clear: defeat the terrorists, free the hostages, and get his wife back. In the end, he does them all, but the emphasis is definitely on dealing with Hans and his gang. And yet, he could have just walked away from all this had his wife not been a hostage, so the heart of the story is the relationship.

In *Life as We Know It*, the Katherine Heigl and Josh Duhamel characters are tasked with taking care of a little girl together. Though that is ostensibly the focus of the film, the real story is their romance and how it will take off and eventually influence what appears to be their primary goal as a couple. In fact, since it is a romantic comedy, the "B" story has become the "A" story—the more important story—and the "A" story, the taking care of the child, has become the "B" story.

Okay, confused yet? Because there's a "C" story in most every film, too. That's the story of the character's change, what most people call the "character arc." Obviously, this story goes hand in hand with the others, but it's a good idea to have a clear grasp of 1) what the character's flaw is; 2) when they realize that flaw; and 3) how they overcome that flaw in the final challenge (the climax).

Assignment

1. Read over the last five pages you wrote of your screenplay. Make changes if necessary.
2. Write five more pages of your screenplay. You should be near the end of act I. Is there an event that compels your protagonist to make a decision to take action?
3. Do you have scenes that focus on the central emotional relationship? If you're not sure with whom your protagonist has a central emotional relationship, think about it this way: With whom do they need to create or repair a relationship in order to reach their goal? This could be the relationship that has to be viable in order for your protagonist to emotionally survive. If it's a love story or a buddy movie, you've got it easy. If it's another kind of picture and you're still not sure, think about your character: Do they not have an important relationship? Why not? That "why not" would be something that your protagonist would have to overcome regarding someone new or returning to their life. Making that relationship happen should be important to your story and important to the protagonist's arc. And resolving it should happen before or during the final challenge of the "A" story.

Lesson Seven

A LOOK AT ALTERNATIVE STRUCTURES

Can you tell a story backward and still have traditional structure? Does it matter if the story you tell is compelling?

Memento—a study in reverse structure.

Okay, you might ask, how the hell is he going to analyze *this* screenplay? A better question might be, *why* the hell is he going to analyze this screenplay? The whole thing is backward, except for the parts that are forward. The scenes begin with the end and end at the beginning. There are scenes in black-and-white that progress in the normal, chronological order, while scenes in color play out in reverse order.

At first glance, this film appears to break most of the rules we've been discussing, and, as such, serves as a reminder that the rules come from without and not from within. That once you know them and have control over them, you can certainly put them aside and follow your own drummer, so long as you are compelling. And I found *Memento*, screenplay by Christopher Nolan based on a short story by Jonathan Nolan, compelling. It kept me guessing all the way to the end, and I'm still wondering 1) did Leonard kill the right person(s); and 2) did he kill his wife?

Of course, for the structure of the movie, it doesn't really matter who killed whom. Leonard's goal is the same. His growth and change are the same. And his future is the same.

Let's start at the beginning. Or the end. Or both. The film itself opens with the last point in the story, when Leonard waves a picture of the man he's just shot. The scene is literally played in reverse, cranked backward so that we're told right up front not to expect traditional structure. In effect, the protagonist has attained his goal in this scene, or, at least, he thinks he has.

The beginning at the end (not *of* the end) is when Leonard burns pictures of himself and Jimmy. He wants to forget what Teddy told him and made him do. He writes down Teddy's license number and admits he'll lie to himself to be happy.

If the inciting incident as seen from the beginning is when Leonard says "I found you, you fuck" after matching the tattooed facts with facts on paper about Teddy, then, if viewed in reverse, the inciting incident at the end would be when he kills Jimmy Grant and changes clothes with him. Everything that happens after that (before that, depending on how you look at the film) is as a result of this action. He's killed the man he took to be his wife's killer, but he knowingly lets himself forget this. Once forgotten, and the picture burned, and Teddy's license written down, he's on a course that must take him to Natalie and her manipulation of events that leads to the beginning (end) when Leonard kills Teddy—whom Natalie wants dead and whom Leonard thinks killed his wife.

Dizzy yet?

The end of act I, seen from the beginning of the film, might be (and I say that because I'm imposing my rules from the outside, I don't know what the Nolans had in mind) when Natalie tells Leonard she lost someone to a guy named Teddy (which she doesn't know is not true). She asks Leonard what he's going to do when he finds John G. He says he'll kill him. She offers to help find him, but the man she's going to help him find is Teddy.

If there's a midpoint in this film, it's probably the midpoint in Sammy Jankis's story when Leonard, before his wife's death, meets with Jankis's wife and tells her there's no physical reason for Sammy's condition. That sends the black-and-white story, in the hotel room, before the killing-of-Jimmy story, into a new direction. Immediately Leonard gets into his (Jimmy's) Jag and Teddy warns him about Natalie, who, in the end, is the one who supplies the information to Leonard that gets Teddy killed.

The end of act II, as long as we're still spitballing about this, is when he tells Natalie the story of the rape/murder. One of the assailants knocks Leonard out, and he lies next to his wife, who is wrapped in a shower curtain. All is lost.

The resolution is the beginning is the end. Leonard learns from Teddy, if we are to believe Teddy, that Sammy never had a wife. That Leonard is the one who administered lethal insulin doses to his wife, who had survived the rape. Leonard's already killed the attacker, he just doesn't remember having done so. Leonard doesn't want to hear this, burns the pictures of him and Jimmy, and admits that he'll lie to himself to be happy. "Now, where am I?"

And we haven't even really discussed what's going on with the black-and-white scenes. They form strange interludes going forward in chronological order, as opposed to the rest of the film. In them, we see the fresh tattoos. We hear Leonard talking on the phone with somebody. We see him get dressed in clothes that are different from the ones in color scenes. We learn about Sammy Jankis's story, in the usual order, the one we're used to. And we see Leonard venture out in his own clothes. In effect, this part of the movie is really just the first fifteen minutes of the story before the story portrayed in the color scenes but played in chronological order. The events that follow the black-and-white scenes take place in color in reverse order.

All right, the viewer has a lot of work to do in this movie. Is it worth it? Of course, that's always up to the viewer, but we can all empathize with someone in a confusing situation where he should, but doesn't, recognize people. It's like a massive alcohol-induced blackout.

We may not have experienced it, but we understand it. We also understand questioning the concepts of identity, memory, and personality. The film offers insight into all of these. And in the end, it also offers purpose to a life that would have no purpose even if memory did serve.

A challenging film and an intellectual puzzle. But did it move you? What do we feel for Leonard? Natalie? Teddy? We're so busy trying to make sense of the story, we find Leonard's emotional journey hard to follow. And isn't the emotional journey why we watch a film?

So if I advocate sticking to the conventional structure, telling a story from the beginning to the end instead of from the end to the beginning, why have I just analyzed *Memento* so fully? Because there is no one way to tell a story. Right now, it's a good idea to tell your story from the beginning to the end, but once you have command of the format, feel free to experiment any way you want. You might end up with something like *Everything Everywhere All at Once*, which blew my mind.

THE *OTHER* PARADIGM—AN ANALYSIS OF *STAR WARS*

The genre sometimes will dictate which format to use or how to order your story. Quest movies lend themselves to the mythic hero's journey, another Hollywood favorite structure. I'm not the first one to point out that the original *Star Wars* (written by George Lucas) follows the paradigm of the mythic hero's journey delineated in Joseph Campbell's *The Hero with a Thousand Faces*. It became so well-known in the industry that George Lucas used the structure that Campbell had described that Campbell's book became required reading for film critics and film analysts. Campbell himself became the subject of so much attention outside of academia that Campbell even sat for several interviews with television journalist Bill Moyers. Linda Seger, in *Making a Good Script Great*, points out that the mythic tale of the hero can be broken down into ten points, according to Campbell. She uses *Star Wars* throughout her book to illustrate the point.

Let's look at *Star Wars: Episode IV—A New Hope*, then, as exemplifying another way to structure a film. Many of the plot points coincide with the structure we've already discussed, and I'll point that out as we go along. While I'll draw on Seger's analysis, I'll focus on a twelve-point structure, described in Christopher Vogler's book *The Writer's Journey: Mythic Structure for Writers*, to illustrate my points.

Just as in all the movies we've looked at, Lucas opens *Star Wars* with views of **ordinary life**. Of course, ordinary life in this case begins with Princess Leia being captured by the forces of the Empire. She sends a pair of androids on a mission to find Obi-Wan Kenobi. Eventually, the droids end up at the farm where Luke Skywalker, his aunt, and his uncle live. This truly is ordinary life, far from the battles of the Empire and the rebel forces. Luke is itching to break away and train to be a pilot, but his prospects are bleak. This is step number one.

Then, while cleaning R2-D2, he receives a hint of his **call to adventure** (step 2) in the form of a hologram of Princess Leia asking Obi-Wan Kenobi for help. It's not the complete call at this stage, since the message is not complete. It's not until he is rescued by Obi-Wan (Ben) Kenobi that he finally hears the whole message. Kenobi then tries to recruit him for the mission he must undertake.

But Luke turns him down. This is the third stage, **the refusal of the call**. The fourth stage, wherein **a mentor encourages him to accept the call**, begins when Kenobi prevails upon him to at least take him partway to Alderaan. When Luke returns to his farm, he finds that stormtroopers have slaughtered his family. He decides to **cross the first threshold and enter the special world**. That's the fifth stage of the story.

Let's stop for a minute and look at this from the point of view of the structure we've been discussing up until now. Yes, we typically start in ordinary life, though we want that to be interesting, too. Then there's an inciting incident that changes the life of the central character forever. In this case, it's the capture of the princess, which leads to the message being sent, which leads to, eventually, Luke's aunt and uncle's death, which leads to his life being changed forever. The goal is set up—he must see that the plans are delivered to the rebel leaders.

Luke crosses the threshold when he begins his search for a ship to take them to the planet where the rebel leaders are. In traditional three-act structure, he's gathering his team for action. Once he has his team, he begins to implement his plan, which is the start of act II. Here, he faces tests almost immediately when they go to the spaceport and enter the bar. This is stage six, and the longest of the stages, wherein **the hero encounters tests, gains allies, and faces enemies**.

With Han Solo joining the team, they are ready for their mission. They encounter problems even before they can take off, but Han proves to be a worthy addition to the team, and they escape.

Luke begins his training in the ways of the Force, and he brings his personal journey into focus. He must learn how to use the Force, how to trust the Force, how to let it enter him so that he can direct it for good. Obi-Wan Kenobi, the mentor, teaches him how to use the light saber, but also instructs him in the ways of his religion. Luke is on the way to becoming a Jedi Knight.

Paralleling act II in traditional structure, this is the longest section of the film. Many challenges confront them. And they face a turning point. Just when they think they've reached their goal, they find that it has been destroyed. And they're sucked into the Death Star. This is the seventh stage, where they **approach the inmost cave, crossing another threshold**. They are still in act II until they escape into the garbage chute. There, Luke is pulled underwater by the garbage monster, and all appears to be lost. It's **the supreme ordeal** of stage eight and the all is lost point of the end of act II, especially when the walls move in to crush Luke and his team.

We're well into act III as they try to flee the ship with the princess. Here, stage nine, **taking possession of the reward**, begins. Luke swings across an abyss with Leia, initiating this stage, which is completed when they all (except Obi-Wan Kenobi) escape, carrying the information (in R2-D2) that the rebels need.

But they are pursued by Imperial fighters on the road back to their (in this case Leia's) ordinary world. This is the beginning of stage ten, **the road back**. The pursuit is more pernicious than it seems. A homing device planted on the ship will lead the Death Star to the planet where the rebels make their central base.

It's at this point that Han Solo's arc becomes important. He's said he's in it for the money, and he means it. Leia replies that if that's all he loves, that's all he'll get.

The Death Star approaches the rebel planet, and the rebels plan the counterattack. This is going to be the big conflict of the third act by one way of reckoning. And once they commit to the battle, and Luke is in a fighter on his way to the Death Star, he has crossed the third threshold. In this eleventh stage, Luke will experience **a resurrection and a transformation**. Now, this becomes a little confusing in *Star Wars* because it is Han's character that is resurrected when he comes to Luke's aid, but it's Luke's that is transformed, with the help of Obi-Wan's voice, into a true Jedi Knight. He lets the Force guide and help him, and thus defeats the enemy. And the Force will be with him always.

The closing sequence is **the return with the elixir** (stage twelve), wherein the hero is recognized as the hero by whomever is important to him. His triumphant moment is the return to tranquility and a new life. Here, Luke, Han, and Chewbacca are recognized as heroes for having saved the rebel planet. Presumably (and as we see in subsequent episodes), life will be different for all of them now that they've gone through the changes brought about by their journey.

Is it better to look at a film, or construct a film, this way, or is the traditional three-act play a more meaningful method of analysis? That depends entirely on the film. You probably could look at any of the Superman or Batman films in this way and find the twelve points. On the other hand, it probably wouldn't work for *Animal*, *Pig*, *The Little Mermaid*, or even *A Beautiful Mind*. It's a form that works best for heroic action films. And if it's used to support the story in that type of film, it can lend the resonance of myth that can only strengthen the impact of the movie.

Assignment

1. Review the structure of your screenplay. Would a twelve-point mythic structure work better for your story than the three-act structure? It's not too late to change, but proceed with caution. Even action-adventure movies work well with the seven-point structure. On the other hand, you can analyze *The Wizard of Oz* using a mythic structure. At this stage in your career, it might be better to stick with the seven points, but I wouldn't rule out the twelve points for future projects.
2. Read over the last five pages you wrote in your screenplay. Make changes if necessary.
3. Then write five more pages of your screenplay. Make sure the challenges to the progress of your protagonist are increasingly more difficult. How's the "B" story coming along? Are there enough scenes focused on that so we care about the central emotional relationship?
4. In your writers group, discuss how a change of structure might enhance your film. Or distract from it.

Lesson Eight

DEEP IN THE MIDDLE OF SOMEWHERE

What is the midpoint? Why is it sometimes called the turning point? Sure, it can come in the middle, and usually does, but it doesn't have to. It's simply a point in the drama, usually midway through, when the action takes an unexpected turn, forcing the story to spin off in a new direction. Let's look at the midpoint in *Unforgiven*, written by David Webb Peoples.

The western is a unique American genre that, like other American forms, has been adapted and amplified by other national cinemas. Sergio Leone and Akira Kurosawa come to mind as directors who have taken the form and made it their own, though it takes some analysis to expose the influence of the western in Kurosawa. Leone made his name with spaghetti westerns—more or less traditionally wrought westerns shot in Italy and Spain that featured modern techniques and stories and, in several of them, Clint Eastwood.

Eastwood, who entered films as an actor in the mid-fifties (with roles in such memorable films as *Francis in the Navy*), cut his acting teeth as a cowboy on TV's *Rawhide*. He later studied at the foot of the master when he acted in Leone's *The Good, the Bad and the Ugly*, *A Fistful of Dollars*, and *For a Few Dollars More*. Eastwood's *High Plains Drifter* more or less followed in the footsteps of Leone. Every few years or so since, he's gone back to the genre to see what is left in the mine. Finally, in 1992, he directed *Unforgiven*, written by David Webb Peoples. Why this script, when he clearly had the choice of any in town? Possibly because the story was more of an anti-western than a traditional western.

Unforgiven features a man whose past is full of the most despicable acts, compounded by alcoholism. But instead of telling a story of redemption, as a normal script would by following the progress of a likeable guy who has gone wrong but then finds his way, Peoples chose to tell the story of an unlikeable guy who had already reformed, who had already redeemed himself, and was already living the life of the righteous man.

What, then, Peoples must have asked, can I throw in this man's path to test him? And what will happen to him when everything goes bad?

We meet William Munny as he buries his wife. Shot from a distance, it's a remote scene, emblematic of Munny's stoicism. In marked contrast, we immediately jump to the town of Big Whiskey, where a cowboy gone crazy (presumably on booze) cuts up a prostitute. Because of the inadequate frontier justice dispensed by Little Bill, the sheriff, her fellow prostitutes gather together and offer up a reward for the perpetrators. This reward drives the story, but it is not strictly the inciting incident. That awaits us until after we really meet William Munny, knee-deep in pig shit and mud trying to separate the hogs with fever from the healthy ones.

He's a dirt farmer, poor as they come, with two kids to raise on his own. We know nothing of what he once was until the Schofield Kid comes a callin'. Schofield, a young gunslinger wannabe, wants to recruit Munny to help kill the cowboys and collect the reward. Munny initially refuses. He's not like that now, meaning he doesn't kill, doesn't drink, doesn't treat animals cruelly. But, confronted with the sick pigs and no money in sight, he takes off after the Kid, first stopping to recruit Ned (the Morgan Freeman character), who used to ride with him in the old days. To Ned, he admits that he regrets his past. He was "one crazy son of a bitch." Only reason he'll do this now, kill these cowboys, is for the money.

So, is he likeable? I don't know. We're confused by this character. He's likeable because he's reformed, he has kids, he'll do anything to take care of them. But he's not likeable because that includes murder for hire. There's no passion in the plan for killing these cowboys, it's not for vengeance, though the Kid tries to get Munny worked up over it, and to a certain extent that's a factor. But the truth is, it's money.

The situation in town is established when English Bob arrives on the train with his biographer, W. W. Beauchamp. When Bob refuses to surrender his gun to a deputy, the confrontation leads to Little Bill doling out a beating. This is to serve as a warning to other gunslingers looking to get the reward, and it tells the audience what dangers might confront Munny if he should enter the town.

Meanwhile, Ned and Munny are ambushed by the Kid, who turns out to be a terrible shot. After some time, they decide on a three-way split for the reward money. In traditional terms, the team has been brought together, and the plan is set. The first act comes to a close, and they ride off into the second act.

Their first obstacle in the second act is that the Kid can't see very well. They adjust their strategy around that and ride on.

The next important scene is back in jail, where we learn of the stuff that Little Bill (the Gene Hackman character) is made of. Yes, we've seen him beat the shit out of English Bob. Now we see him give a gun to Beauchamp and tell him to shoot him (Little Bill). We all discover how it's not so easy to kill a man. We also discover that Little Bill has nerves of steel. Bob refuses to shoot him, though he'd have the drop on him.

As Munny and his entourage reach town, they see English Bob riding out on the train. Little Bill has commandeered Beauchamp's services as biographer and tells him how it "really" is. He also makes sure we know "I do not like assassins. Men of no character." We know the confrontation is coming.

At the "billiard" house, Will Munny doesn't go upstairs for an "advance" on his reward like Ned and the Kid do. When deputies enter, and Will denies carrying a gun, he, too, is beaten. In the fracas, Ned and the Kid escape out the windows, and Will eventually crawls out the door. But it's still not personal, even when Ned and the Kid are sewing up Will. A stoic, Will is driven only by money.

Next morning, Ned and the Kid argue about leaving Will behind. "He ain't nothin' but a broke down pig farmer," the Kid argues, perhaps rightly. But Ned is loyal, and he's not about to do that to his friend. He nurses him through his fever and notes Will's wish that his kids not know what he'd done before he met their mother.

Will finally comes out of his delirium, helped by the cut prostitute. In another character-building moment, we see him turn down a chance to collect an advance on his reward "on account of my wife."

It's back, now, to the task at hand. They ambush the cowboys, and Will, missing a few times, finally kills one of them. But the experience reminds Ned why he gave up gunslinging, and he pulls out of the deal.

Lots has happened up to this point, most of which has been set up for things to come. The only obstacle has been the confrontation in the billiard house, but it really hasn't stopped them from achieving at least part of their goal. But now Will is without his partner. He's left with an untried, unpredictable kid. Things are going to be different.

This is the midpoint, the turning point of the film. Things are going in a new direction now for two reasons: Ned's gone, and Little Bill forms a posse to find who killed the cowboys. These actions lead to deputies finding Ned on the trail and bringing him in, while the Kid and Will sneak up on the ranch. It also sets in motion events that will return the story, in part, to more traditional themes.

The whole town stops as Little Bill whips Ned. It looks like Ned won't talk.

Meanwhile, back at the ranch (always wanted to say that), the Kid finally shoots a cowboy who's gone to the outhouse unchaperoned. It's hard to get away from the ranch, especially when Will's horse won't hold still, but they escape. Then the Kid finally admits it was his first kill, and he's a wreck. Munny's answer to this is simply, "It's a helluva thing killing a man. Take away all he's got and all he's ever gonna have." To which the Kid replies, "I guess he had it comin'." Will's rejoinder is only, "We all have it comin', Kid." In other words, the end is inevitable.

Things are definitely not going as planned. When the prostitute brings them the reward money, she tells them Ned's dead and that he talked before he died. This is the low point of the film. The all is lost point. Now it's not about the money anymore. It's about revenge and survival. They know Will's name. He must take action according to the code of the west, which is precisely why Little Bill puts Ned's body on display.

Now we can have sympathy for Munny because money no longer is driving his actions. Now he's driven by loyalty. Now it's good guy against bad guy again. There are fewer moral ambiguities. The sheriff has done him wrong (and will really do him wrong if he catches him).

What does a reformed alcoholic do when confronted by seemingly insurmountable odds? This one drinks again. We know that Will has admitted to doing lots of despicable acts when drunk in the past. We can only imagine what will happen now. But we know he must do them. How do we feel about Will? Probably conflicted. We admire his loyalty, yet he is a killer. The Kid, on the other hand, turns out to be tremendously shaken by the killing experience and gives his rifle to Will. The killing has changed his life for the better. Will sends him off with the money to give to his kids, and Will rides into town, setting up the final confrontation—a battle of Wills (Little Bill versus Will Munny).

Little Bill has put Ned's body on display in front of the billiard hall/saloon, and Will enters the bar with his shotgun ready. In a room full of deputies, and Little Bill, he fires and kills the bar's owner, Skinny, for decorating his saloon with his friend. Then he turns the shotgun on Little Bill, but it misfires. But that doesn't stop his rage. He throws the shotgun at Bill and then kills him and several others with his pistol. Within moments he's killed everyone who needs killing and spared everyone who doesn't. He leaves the living to bury the dead, and they don't bother him on the way out.

The film closes with him returning to visit his wife's grave, presumably to ask forgiveness and to go on with his life.

The turning point can be the moment the central character changes (and changes his goal or plan), or it can be just the opportunity for change. It can change the whole direction of a movie or just point in that direction. Think of Howard at the crossroads in *In & Out*. Think of Will Munny when he learns of Ned's death. These are turning points in the central character's journey, and thus turning points in the film's story.

A NEW KIND OF BUDDY FILM

Who's the main character in a buddy film? Isn't this genre, by definition, a story about two people? So how can we say one is the protagonist? And if we do, what is the other?

Think about a romantic comedy for a second. Isn't it always mainly about one person in the couple? Isn't one the object of the pursuit, while the other is the pursuer? In *Shakespeare in Love*, it's pretty obvious (in case the title didn't tell you). How about *Sleepless in Seattle*? Less obvious. But it's really the Meg Ryan character who does the pursuing, who has the goal. And that's the key—who has the goal, who goes through the arc, who is different in the end than they were in the beginning?

Let's look again at *Thelma & Louise*, screenplay by Callie Khouri. When it first came out, it was a cultural phenomenon—a female buddy picture with violence at its core. (As an aside, you'll note that the violence is either perpetrated against women, or by women against men who have violated them in some way. The armed robbery isn't violent. In fact, it's very polite.) And the ending is a depressing statement about ____. You fill in the blank.

But is it Thelma's movie or Louise's movie? I must tell you, I had my doubts at first, though the title is always a good place to start. Top billing in the title usually means that's the person who is the center of the picture. Not always, but almost always. But for a long while into the movie, and even when I was first thinking it through after reviewing it, I thought it was Louise's movie. She's the motivator. She seems to propel the action, while Thelma is pulled along by events. And one of the key things a protagonist must do is to drive the action. Louise is the one who takes justice in her hands, she's the one who decides they need to go to Mexico. Hell, it was her idea to go on the vacation in the first place. Isn't this story about her?

No. In case you haven't already guessed, it's about Thelma. And it's nowhere near an equal story either, once you understand that 1) Thelma states her goal; 2) the inciting incident (the rape) is a statement of her general condition; 3) Thelma is the one who goes through an arc and changes; and 4) Thelma finally takes charge of things.

Every movie is about a person who has a need to change, struggles with that need, and, against the obstacles in her way, makes the change and comes out (we hope) a better person. Okay, Will Munny is probably no different at the end than he was at the beginning. But Will Shakespeare is better for having loved and lost, Dorothy changed in *The Wizard of Oz*, Howard changed in *In & Out*. It's about the journey. So, what's Thelma's journey?

From a passive wife to an independent armed robber. Maybe not the best way to go in life, but let's take it step by step.

Thelma starts off as the repressed housewife to car salesman district manager Darryl, a pig if there ever was one. (By the way, the actor who played Darryl, Christopher McDonald, had a key supporting role in my first network show, an episode of *The Twilight Zone*, "Aqua Vita." He played a very spooky water delivery man. A novice, he actually asked me and my then writing partner, Jeremy Finch, if it was okay to play the part in a certain way. I say *novice* because most actors would direct their question to the director. We told him yes anyway and were very pleased with the results.) Thelma even has to ask his permission to go away for the weekend. Her first act of rebellion comes when she calls Louise back and tells her the pickup time.

And another "by the way": This is a film full of montages. The first long one is Thelma packing. But the point of this montage is to show her packing way too much stuff (which will lead to conclusions made by the cop, Hal Slocumb, much later), and to note that she packs a gun with distaste. How she handles the gun later will also demonstrate how far she's come on her journey.

Once she's in the car, and has handed over the gun to Louise, she hears some fateful words: "You get what you settle for." Apparently, she's settled for Darryl. If she ever wants to get rid of him, we infer, she's got to do something about it.

Then there's montage number two—travel—at the end of which they make a stop at a country bar and Thelma tells us her goal. She wants to "get out of town and, for once, really let our hair down." And the drinking begins. Louise is a little hesitant, but Thelma reminds her, "You said we were gonna have some fun, so let's have some." Thelma starts dancing with a stranger who fills her full of beer and spins her 'til she's dizzy. When he takes her outside for some "air," he forces himself on her. Soon, it's a full-fledged rape and beating, eventually stopped by Louise pulling the trigger of Thelma's gun and putting a hole in the man's heart.

Now that's an inciting incident!

Their lives are definitely going to change now. They get the hell outta there and hit the road. They don't know what they want to do, but Louise quickly nixes the idea of going to the police. She's got to figure out what to do next. Now, so far, Thelma's been pulled by the action. It looks like Louise is in charge here, but it's only because of what has happened to Thelma that the story gets going in the first place. Louise spends a lot of time reminding us she needs to figure out what to do. Eventually, she asks her boyfriend, Jimmy, to wire her her life's savings. She's got a plan. When they split from the first hotel, that's the end of act I.

But, you say, *Louise* is the one with the plan, so isn't she the protagonist? It would seem so, on the surface. Though she's the one with a goal at first, she hasn't made any progress toward a change. Let's look at Thelma. She's called Darryl at four in the morning, and he wasn't there. She starts to understand that maybe she's the one who should be upset about her spouse's behavior instead of vice versa. After Louise decides they should go to Mexico, Thelma has a conversation with Darryl, but he's too busy with his football game. He makes an idle threat, and she tells him to "go fuck yourself." Her attitude is changing.

And it's going to change even more, we see, when she stumbles over J.D., played by Brad Pitt. She turns him down when he tries to hitch a ride but eventually gets Louise to stop for him. Before that, however, she decides to go to Mexico and learns about Louise's past run-in with the law in Texas.

Meanwhile, Hal Slocumb, played by Harvey Keitel, is getting closer and closer to their trail, still treating them as witnesses, but also as possible suspects, in the shooting. He enlists Darryl to help him.

Jimmy's waiting for Louise at the hotel where he was supposed to wire her the money. She gives the money to Thelma for safekeeping, and we *should* know by now that something's going to go wrong with that, but we don't. When J.D. comes to her door, all wet and seductive, Thelma takes him in, and her life really changes. She and Darryl have been together since she was fourteen. He is the only man she's ever known. Now she learns a thing or two about sex with J.D. As a matter of fact, she's lightheaded and drunk with sex the next morning. That is, until Louise asks her where the money is. J.D. has stolen it. Now the story spins off in a new direction. Thelma wants to maintain that "It's okay," but Louise says, "It's not okay. None of this is okay."

Still, Thelma is pulled along by events. She hasn't yet propelled the action by design, though what has happened to her has propelled the action. But now she has to take action. They're on the lam, and they haven't got any money. One thing J.D. did leave her was a lesson in how to rob a convenience store. When they make a stop, she repeats his lesson verbatim in the store, and finally Thelma has taken charge of her own life. It may not be the best course, but at least she's making her own decisions for a change.

Of course, Darryl can't believe it when the FBI and Hal show him the tape, but Thelma thinks she may have "found her calling" (armed robbery). Hal later questions J.D. and asks him if he thinks Thelma would have robbed the store if he hadn't stolen their money, and it's clear he thinks they're just victims of circumstance. When Louise and Thelma next call Darryl, Louise asks him to put the cops on, and Hal takes the phone. He wants them to turn themselves him; he knows they're going to Mexico.

This is the low point of the film, the end of the second act. Nothing's going well. And now the cops know where they're headed. They're frightened but determined. They head off into the night.

Next morning, they're harassed by a trucker, then pulled over by a state trooper. The trooper takes Louise into his car, and it looks like he's going to find out who they are when Thelma again takes charge of the situation and forces him into his trunk at gunpoint. As they head out of state, Louise regrets not going to the cops in the first place (and we wonder, again, why they didn't, no matter what she had to hide about previous shootings). But it's too late. Still, she calls Slocumb, who tries to talk her into coming in. Her answer—"Do I want to come out alive? I don't know. I'm gonna have to think about that"—foreshadows a dark ending. We can see she's made a decision, though.

Strangely, Thelma is now worried that Louise will make a deal. Thelma says she can't go back, she can't go back to that life. She feels awake for the first time. She has something to look forward to.

When the trucker harasses them again, they teach him a lesson, but they don't harm him. They're not really violent, the writer is telling us. They only react with violence when forced to. And even then, they avoid hurting anyone when they can.

But now they've been located, and the final chase is on. Thelma tells Louise she is a good friend, and the premise of the movie is set out for us: True friendship survives anything, even death. (Similar to *Romeo and Juliet*—true love survives anything, even death.) On the edge of the Grand Canyon, with no escape possible, Louise says she's not going to give up. Thelma suggests that they don't get caught. They should keep on goin'. She points to the edge of the canyon. Louise: "You sure?" Thelma: "Yeah." They kiss, start the car, hold hands, and fly into the canyon.

Yep, they had the time of their lives. And now their lives are over. But Thelma went on an incredible journey of self-discovery and change. Louise already knew who she was. And that's how Khouri chose her protagonist—by deciding who needed to go on this journey wherein two women discover true friendship and leave all the men in their lives behind. Once the characters were created, the focus was inevitable.

The answer to the question "If Thelma is the protagonist, what is Louise?" is probably that Louise is the catalyst. Without her, none of this would have happened. She has to be present for the change to happen, just like a catalyst in a chemical reaction. She is also the central emotional relationship person, a key character in any film.

If you have the inclination, take a look at *Butch Cassidy and the Sundance Kid*. Not only are the two characters equally represented, they even fall in love with the same woman. Now, who is the protagonist in that picture?

Assignment

1. You should be getting close to the midpoint in your film. Many things can happen at the midpoint: Your protagonist can realize what their flaw is and decide to try to overcome it. Your protagonist can face an event that causes them to change their plan. They wanted something at the end of act I—the goal. At this point, they *need* something more crucial in their life. Have you changed your protagonist's goal from a want to a need?
2. Read over the last five pages you wrote in your screenplay. Make changes if necessary.
3. Write five more pages of your screenplay, making sure there is rising conflict (more and more difficult barriers to your protagonist's goals). Start aiming at the midpoint change.
4. In your writers group, discuss what you want your audience (or reader) to feel at the conclusion of your film. Is the ending satisfying? How does it compare to the ending of *Thelma & Louise*?

Lesson Nine

SOME TECH THINGS YOU SHOULD KNOW

The script, whether in television, streaming, feature films, or even the internet, is a technical document as much as it is an artistic work. It's what up to two hundred people (and more, if there are a lot of special effects or huge crowd scenes) depend on to know what to do. There are a few things you can do to make your script easier for your production manager, cinematographer, and director to read and produce.

First thing is to let everyone do their jobs. That means keep descriptions of the camera angles and moves to a minimum. (There are ways to do that subliminally, but that's fodder for another time.) Don't delineate in detail what's on the walls of a luxury apartment (the production designer, art director, and props person will decide that). Don't tell us the color of the flowers on the ingenue's dress. We don't need to know what kind of shoes she's wearing, either, unless it's important for the story or character (like that she wears flat sandals to a formal wedding—that would say something about her. But that she wears shoes to match her dress—not needed).

We also don't need to know how the sun's rays filter through the curtains, so long as you tell us the time of day. We don't need to know the wind is blowing at fifteen miles per hour or what kind of car the taxi is, unless, again, it's important to the story.

So details, except those that define the character, you can skip.

But first, a word from our slugline master. Why do we include INT. and EXT.? Because we need to know what lights to order and how to schedule the shoot. Used to be that would determine what kind of film to order as well, but since hardly anyone is using film, that's mostly irrelevant (video you can adjust on the fly). The next words in the slug should be the exact location, i.e., JOE'S APARTMENT. The next word is simply the time of day, and that also has to do with lighting, even in interiors: DAY or NIGHT. LATER doesn't mean a damn thing when the UPM is breaking down the script or the DP and gaffer are going over the schedule and trying to figure out what lights to order for the next day. And it's *always* later, isn't it? Except, of course, in *Memento,* in which case it's always earlier (in the "in color" parts of the story). So don't use LATER.

CONTINUOUS doesn't cut it either. One exception: if the action moves fluidly from one location to another with the camera or a cut that's almost invisible. For instance, if you move from inside the house to outside the house, that's a continuous action. Just because one scene happens after another does not make it continuous. Just because one scene happens at the same time as another does not make it continuous. Yes, you will see this on some scripts, and, yes, you will see LATER, too, but that doesn't mean the writers are using it correctly. They may think they are, and everyone up the ladder may think they are, but the UPM will be pissed when they try to board (or schedule) that scene. Is that a day shoot or a night shoot? Later? How much later? How does that make a difference? Is it day or night?

Yes, you can use MORNING or EVENING, or even DAWN. But not MOMENTS LATER. You show *that* in what follows by including some change in the description.

Speaking of description, don't forget to follow each slugline with a short description of who's there and what they are doing. Don't follow the slugline with a line of dialogue. People need to know who's in the scene, maybe what they're wearing, and especially what they're doing. If you jump right into dialogue, and, for example, they shoot that scene another day instead of shooting it the same day as the previous scene, nobody is going to know where to stand or what to be doing.

Make everything clear for everyone. But give them creative input. One well-known book on directing tells the director, and by implication the actors, to cross out all the action lines in a scene. That might be going a little too far, but don't overdirect in your script (have a look at Joe Eszterhas's *Basic Instinct* for an extremely lean script in terms of description). Give your actors room to interpret. That's their job. That means, too, that you should keep your parenthetical expressions to a minimum. Only put in something that can't be inferred from the dialogue, such as SARCASTICALLY or SOTTO. And keep actions to action lines. In other words, this would not be good:

```
                    JOE
            (Walking over to Pete
            slowly and wringing his
            hands in despair)
      Help me! I'm stuck in an amateur script,
      and I can't get out.
```

Yes, in TV, the rules are a little different if you're on staff and almost talking directly to the director or actors. Yes, you can get away with more when you're rich and famous. Yes, you will see bad examples of all of the above in good scripts. No, you're not rich and famous, so you need to do it the right way.

Assignment

1. Read over the last five pages you wrote in your screenplay. Are you trying to direct it on the page? Are you including camera moves? Did you describe the wallpaper? Make sure your pages are succinct and clear. Make changes if necessary.
2. Write five more pages of your screenplay.
3. In your writers group, try switching around the people who have been playing your characters to see if different voices improve your pages. You may find something with different readers. Does that help your dialogue?

Lesson Ten

THE PUKE DRAFT

What is a puke draft? It's the one that flows out willy-nilly, sometimes formless, raw, or spontaneous. It's the purest form, undisturbed by your own censor or anyone else's comments. It's the way you should write the first draft of your screenplay and anything else you write.

But as if that's not hard enough to do, once you're done with that draft, you've got to start the rewrite process. Here's where the craft comes in, where you analyze the dialogue, weigh the acts, follow the plotlines, and check for sense and continuity.

Usually, the first draft is too long, and a few judicious cuts will help the pacing. Look for scenes that don't tell you anything new, that don't move the action forward. Then cut them. Yes, cut them. Look for couplets (dialogue pairs—one person talks, another responds, once each) that repeat parts of the conversation. Look for scenes that lack conflict or, in the case of a comedy, just aren't funny. Then cut them.

Assignment

1. With any luck, you should be at the midpoint of your script by now. If you're not, get there. If you're there, congratulations, you're about halfway through the puke draft.

2. This is a good time to check your page count. There is no law that says you need a certain number of pages in your script, but the norm is 95–105. Anything much shorter is probably not well-enough developed, though technically, according to the Academy of Motion Picture Arts and Sciences, a feature only needs to be forty minutes. That would be fine for a half hour pilot, which usually runs long on the page, but unless your film has no dialogue, aim for the norm. Are you halfway there? Great!
3. Take a deep breath and go on to the next lecture.
4. But first, check in with your writers group. Are people keeping up? What challenges are they (or you) facing? Have you reached a turning point in your story?

Course 3

INTRODUCTION TO SCREENWRITING III

Perhaps the hardest part of writing a screenplay is finishing. Many writers get stuck in the middle because they didn't work out the story in their treatment, or they have come up with a new idea (or even premise), scene, or character that affects the whole screenplay. Often they write and rewrite and rewrite again without ever finishing a draft. If you've followed all the assignments, you should be able to finish the first draft of your screenplay by the end of this third course. Yes, you may come up with some new ideas. You may decide to change the gender of your protagonist. You may have a different idea for the midpoint. Make a note of these ideas but continue on the path you outlined in your beat sheet and treatment.

I understand that every writer has their own process, and yours may be different from mine. You may want to make significant changes at any stage, and that's all right. But at some point you have to decide that those changes can be made in the next draft so you can actually finish the current draft. Try to avoid the change-everything cycle that would prevent you from finishing a draft. You'll be glad you did.

Lesson One

WHO WE ARE

Are you a screenwriter? If we define a screenwriter as someone who has *completed* a screenplay, then, if you aren't already, you will be by the end of this class. One of the most important things you can do as a screenwriter is meet other screenwriters, so try to establish relationships (network) with others in a writing group. You'll need support from other screenwriters often in your career, and this is a good place to create that support system.

One thing you'll need that support system for is to have people who don't want something from you read your work and give you honest criticism (notes). Your mom, bless her heart, your significant other, your friends—all want to help, but they also want to make you feel good (or bad, depending on what kind of friends they are). They also probably don't know how to give you a constructive suggestion because they're not screenwriters.

So, what do you want to hear from people who read your work?

The truth.

Delivered in the most positive-sounding way.

When you write notes for your classmates, keep in mind how you would want to read notes on your own screenplay. Start off with something that worked for you. Then point out areas that could use improvement. If you have an idea on how to help, you can suggest it. A good development exec will stop with pointing out the issues (never use the word *problems*) and will let the writer come up with solutions. But writer to writer, give a brother or sister a break if you can and suggest solutions. Then end on another positive note, and you're done.

One of the reasons I ask for you to criticize each other's work is the hope that you'll develop a critical eye that one day you'll be able to focus on your own work—and remember, it's your work we're talking about here, not you. So nothing personal. Learning how to read another's treatment or script means you'll learn how to read your own more dispassionately. A bonus is you'll have several sharp minds besides my battered one giving you thoughts and opinions. Trust me, some of the best suggestions come from your colleagues.

LAYING THE GROUNDWORK—STRUCTURE

I assume you already have a solid treatment based on the traditional three-act structure. If you've chosen another format (the twelve-point hero's journey, for example), I hope you have a good reason for that. The three-act structure has worked for dramas since before Aristotle codified it in *Poetics*. For good luck, let's review:

1. **Ordinary Life:** getting to know who the central character is and what their issue is.
2. **Inciting Incident:** usually around page fifteen, give or take a couple of pages. This is what changes their life forever. This eventually forces them to act.
3. **End of Act I:** when something happens that compels your character to decide on a goal and a course of action (a plan) in order to deal with whatever the inciting incident brought up. This usually occurs between pages twenty-five and thirty-five.
4. **Midpoint or Turning Point:** Yes, this happens right around the middle wherein the action takes a sudden and new, unexpected

direction. The goal may change. The central character may realize what their flaw is. Instead of what they want, what they need becomes most important.

5. **Low Point:** end of the second act. The all is lost point in terms of the goal. There seems to be no way in hell they'll ever reach their goal. Happens around page seventy-five to eighty, depending on the length of the script.
6. **Final Challenge:** that final test, the final barrier that your character must overcome in order to reach their goal. Very close to the end.
7. **Return to the (Now Changed Forever) Normal Life:** two or three pages to show us that life goes on and that our character has triumphed.

This is only a guideline, of course. But the inciting incident should come as early as you can get it while still showing us who the main character is and why we should care about them. All points after that are **in relation to the character's goal.**

It's worth noting, too, that sequences and even scenes are structured in this way, though sometimes the first and seventh steps are left off in scenes if they are understood.

STORY

It's good, at this point, to remember what the basic definition is of the word *story* for our purposes. Think of it in these terms: There's a person. They have a goal (they want something). There's a rock (a barrier) between them and their goal. They have to go over, under, around, or through the rock to get to the goal.

That process of going over, under, around, or through—that's the story.

Now, review your treatment for structure. Does your treatment fit the paradigm I've described or, if not, do you have a good reason why not (using the mythic structure, for example)?

OPENINGS

I also want you to check your pages for a few things before we go on. Since the key to problems in the second and third acts is often the setup in the first act, I want you to review what you've already written. The first thing we are going to look for is how you've introduced your central character.

It's a good idea to show your central character's flaw in the first visual we have of them. It's the flaw that sets up the need for change, and it's the flaw that the protagonist is going to have to overcome in themself in the final challenge while they deal with the antagonist.

How to do that? In *Die Hard*, written by Jeb Stuart based on the book by Roderick Thorp, we see John McClane grip his airline handrest for dear life: He's afraid of heights. Later, in the final challenge, he has to get over that fear. But that's not all we learn about him in the first few minutes. His ring tells us he's married. He's skeptical. He's a cop. He has at least one kid, and he feels guilty about something (an oversized teddy bear tells us that). He's attracted to other women but doesn't make a move when he could, so he's faithful. He's a little bit cocky (his walk in the airport), and he's a man of the people (never been in a limo before). All this in five minutes. We know his issues, his situation, his personality. We quickly learn the same things about his wife, setting this up as a relationship movie. Yes, it's a romance, disguised as an action flick.

His Girl Friday opens with the setting, then moves quickly to Hildy Johnson as she steps out of the elevator. Immediately we begin a visual lesson in who she is: She's aggressive. She takes charge. She's confident. She walks ahead of her fiancé. She's a professional woman with style. She's the dominant one in the relationship. She's had a bad one before this. She can take care of herself. She's a woman of the people (she talks with the operators). We learn a ton about her both visually and in dialogue in less than five minutes (about five pages).

Platoon, written by Oliver Stone, does the whole introduction without words. We see the raw recruit, Chris Taylor, survey the airport after emerging from the belly of the transport. It's almost as if he's coming out of the birth canal, he's so innocent. But he sees what can happen to him when he views the body bags and the soldiers who are shipping out. Wide-eyed and impressionable, he's about to enter hell without a handbasket.

There is another way to introduce the protagonist using voiceover to tell you exactly who they are, as Robert Pattinson does in 2022's *The Batman*, written by Matt Reeves, Peter Craig, and Bob Kane.

So what I'm saying is go back and check your pages to make sure they introduce a character we care about and that we learn as much as we can about them as quickly as possible to set up the story and to show us that something is going to need to shake up their lives.

Now you're ready to rock. I look forward to reading your new pages.

Just a reminder: Writing takes place when you're staring off into space (something spouses, significant others, and children rarely understand), when you're driving the car, when you're brushing your teeth. Keep pencil and paper handy for notes. You'll be glad you did.

Assignment

1. Complete the script status report on page 162. You will be asked for your premise. I don't mean a summary of your story, but the point you're trying to get across, i.e., "Love conquers all, even death." (Return to lessons one and two in Introduction to Screenwriting I for a review of premise.) The point of the script status report is for you to review where you are in the process and to give you a chance to revise what you have, if necessary.
2. Make any changes to your script that need to be made. This is part of the process. You write. You rewrite. You write again.
3. Write five more pages.
4. In your writers group, discuss everyone's progress—or lack of progress. What's holding them back? What are the secrets of those who are progressing well? Share.

Script Status Report

Your name:

Project name:

What is the premise of your script (idea, not story) in one sentence?

Who is the main character, in one sentence?

What do they think they want? What do they really want?

Who or what is preventing them from achieving that?

What inside of them is preventing them from achieving that?

What do they have to learn about themself? About others?

Who are the other main players? What are their needs?

What is the genre of your script?

What is the everyday life of the protagonist?

What is the inciting incident?

What is the act I curtain?

What is the midpoint?

What is the act II curtain?

What is the final challenge?

What is the return to the (now changed forever) normal life?

What is working?

What is not working?

What must change?

Lesson Two

CONFLICT, CONFLICT, CONFLICT

There, I've said it again. Even something so seemingly devoid of conflict as the opening scene of *Platoon* is full of it—Taylor has to fight the sun and the dust from the moment he steps off the plane. Some conflict is subtext—expectations versus realities. Clean uniforms and fresh faces versus body bags and the hardened faces of the vets shipping out. Everything is in contrast.

Of course, it's easy to put conflict in a fight scene, whether it's a physical fight or a verbal one. Arguments are good sources of conflict. But you don't want to have two hours of argument. It's just tiresome. But people can be in opposition and not be angry. Or they can hide their anger on purpose or unintentionally, or they can be unaware they're angry, or they can just not give a damn, which would frustrate the person with whom they're in opposition. It's all about having different goals and expectations.

Let's look at a scene in *Shakespeare in Love*, screenplay by Marc Norman and Tom Stoppard. This most literate of screenplays features dialogue that flows from the mouths of a number of diverse characters, each with their own voice. Listen carefully to each person speaking—they have different vocabulary, different cadences, not to mention different accents. And despite the fact that it's an extremely talky film, it never gets boring (for me, at least) because there's always conflict.

You could pick almost any scene as an example of good structure and dialogue, but let's look at one that appears near the middle of the movie. In this scene, Wessex announces his impending marriage with Viola as if he has just closed an important business deal. (He has.) There's no asking for her hand, there's no show of love. Strictly business. In case we didn't know Wessex is a prick—we've seen him nearly trample Shakespeare and the musicians outside Viola's house, we've seen him talk to Viola's father about Viola as if she were a prize cow, we've seen him take a knife to Shakespeare's throat—we now hear what kind of man Viola's to wed.

The scene starts with conflict. He bitches at the nurse for Viola's being at prayer for two hours and calls himself Viola's six-day lord and master. We know Viola to be independent and thoughtful, so we know that she's holding in her true feelings when she opens with "You've been waiting" in an apologetic tone. He refuses to be gracious—"I'm aware of it."—though he is, in his mind, complimentary. Of course, he hasn't seen the mustache and small beard that she entered the scene with, and he won't because of some quick thinking by the nurse.

A scene has a beginning, a middle, and an end. It's also constructed just like the screenplay as a whole, with a moment of ordinary life, an inciting incident, an act I curtain, a midpoint (turning point), an act II curtain (all is lost), a final challenge, and a return to normal. This scene has that classic construction. Essex is the protagonist of this scene. He's the one with a goal. He drives the action. The ordinary life is Essex ranting and raving to the nurse. The inciting incident is the arrival of Viola. There's some small talk as he moves toward stating his goal and plan: Essex informs Viola of the marriage contract and his plan to start a tobacco farm. The midpoint is Viola telling him she doesn't love him, followed quickly by the low point when he kisses her, and she slaps him. The final challenge is when he tells her she will be submissive, modest, grateful, and brief. The return to normal is when she capitulates: "I will do my duty, my lord."

Just two minutes long and we know his personality, his plans, her reaction, her sense of duty, and the inevitable outcome.

If the protagonist of a scene has a goal, and the antagonist's job is to thwart that goal, who is the protagonist of this scene? Not the heroine of the movie. No. She enters the scene without a goal, though she soon develops one. The protagonist of the scene is Wessex, as I've said, whose goal is to begin shaping his marriage. Viola fights him at every turn, until, forced by her sense of duty and devotion to her father, she resigns herself to her fate. She uses words, actions, anything she can think of to put him off, but he doesn't care. He needs her—her money and childbearing abilities (so that he can work his estates in Virginia)—too much to let a small thing like contempt stand in the way of his happiness.

No argument in the sense that they're not screaming at each other, but they are opposed. Their goals are in conflict.

Some scenes don't have all the parts of the seven-point structure. It's best to enter a scene as late as possible and leave as soon as you've reached the objective of the scene. That means that sometimes you won't see the bit of implied normal life. You might start with the inciting incident of the scene. Even *that* might be implied, but that's hard to do. It's not at all unusual, especially in television dramas, to leave the scene at the close of the low point to keep suspense going, especially just before a commercial if it's on a traditional network or cable. Watch *Succession, Yellowstone, The Bear*, or *Law & Order* and see if you can pick out 1) the goals of the principal characters; 2) the overall purpose of the scene; and 3) where in the structure the scene began and ended. You'll see many, if not all, of them enter late and leave early.

And have plenty of conflict.

Assignment

1. Write new short character sketches. Ask yourself:
   - Have your characters changed since original conception?
   - How will your characters change in the process of the film?
   - What is your protagonist's flaw?
   - How will they overcome it?
2. Write ten new pages in your screenplay.
3. In your writers group, focus on a scene you're having trouble with. Why is it not working? Is it the setup? Is it the lack of conflict? Are the goals clear?

Lesson Three

ACTION EQUALS CHARACTER

One of the most difficult things to do in film is to show the inner workings of a character's mind. New writers often use voiceover to tell us how a character is feeling or what they plan to do or what they remember about the past. Even worse, some have the characters talk out loud with no one else in the room. Some use the device of talking to a pet or a photo or even a stuffed toy. But all these devices are a clumsy way to tell a story (though even the best of writers sometimes find they must resort to them). What's better? Action.

Action is character. A character defines himself by what he does. We've all heard "It's not what you say, it's what you do," and that's something to keep in mind when writing a screenplay. By *do*, I mean anything that a character does, from the way they hold a toothbrush to the way they sweep across the floor in a waltz. Will Smith's character in *The Pursuit of Happyness* runs a lot, thus underscoring his feeling of urgency. Woody Allen's character in *Annie Hall* shows us his ineptitude in a number of ways when he's trying to wrestle a lobster into a pot. Cate Blanchett's character in *Tár* shows us who she is by the way she conducts an orchestra, no matter where it is. Even HAL 9000 in *2001* shows us who he is by locking doors. They don't have to tell us who they are; they show us by what they do.

There are even subtler ways to convey human emotion without dialogue or on-the-nose description: A character takes frequent bathroom breaks. Another has a tic. A man breaks into a sweat. Tears roll down the cheeks of a child. A woman smiles wryly. A boy tries to work up some moisture in his mouth.

Sure, you could have said the person needing the bathroom was afraid. The one with a tic was worried they'd be found out. The sweating man in a cold room has something to hide. The child may miss their dog. The woman knows more than she is telling. The boy is scared. But by showing us the physical condition, you make it easy on the actor and the reader to almost subliminally understand what's going on.

Some characters can externalize traits via their physicality. A person with a scar across his eyeline hints at a mysterious background. A man who shaves his head is different from one who has shoulder-length hair. A woman who needs a manicure or a man who has one—that's information that tells us something about a person. Their clothes, their apartment, their office, their car—all can say something about character without talking out loud.

On the other hand, sometimes the only way we really know someone is by what they say.

THE DEFINING LINE

Often a movie will have a defining line, something that encapsulates everything the movie is about in just a single sentence. More than that, it succinctly reveals to the audience who the lead character is. The late Jim Schmerer of UCLA's Professional Program in Screenwriting first pointed this out to me.

The defining line also shows that the character knows who they are.

It calls for the use of the pronouns *I, me, my,* or *mine*. Think of Michael in *Tootsie*. He's walking down the street with his agent: "I'm a better man as a woman than I was as a man."

Doesn't that say everything there is to say about him? Doesn't that give us the key to the film?

Finding the line for your central character will help you to know them better. If you know the underlying reasons for why a character acts the way they do, not the plot points or what they do, but *why* they do it, what's inside that character—what's driving them—it impacts each scene in everything they say and do.

If you know this, you will have your audience emotionally involved in the character.

Here's another example. Marlowe in *The Maltese Falcon*. It looks like he'll do anything inside or outside the law to reach his goal—money, the falcon. In the final scene, he turns to the woman he loves and tells her he's going to turn her in for killing his partner.

"Don't believe I'm as crooked as they say. It's good for business." At that moment we know he was a moral detective, and everything was geared toward finding out who killed his partner.

Think of *Dirty Harry*. Of course, you know the one line that defined his character. It was on the tongue of everybody in America. It still is. "Make my day." In three words, he defined his character. He told us he would risk it all to get the bad guy and would kill him gladly. His morality is his own, not society's.

In *Mission Impossible—Dead Reckoning Part One*, written by Christopher McQuarrie and Erik Jendresen, Tom Cruise's character, Ethan Hunt, tells us exactly who he is by using the royal *we*: "We live and die in the shadows for those we hold close, and for those we never meet."

Think of the line your central character would use to define themself, their goal, their purpose. Even if you don't use it in your script (though you probably should), it helps to know what it would be.

ONE MORE THING ABOUT CHARACTERS

Audiences like to watch people they care about, and actors like to play characters that are characters—that's what gets them the Academy Award nominations. The audience needs to care about a character, so you need to show us why they would. You need to make the audience eager to know how things turn out for your protagonist. You need to make it plain what it is about this character that we like or admire or just find interesting.

But do we have to *like* this character? Think about it. How many films are successful that have unredeemed assholes as their central character (other than *Scarface* or *The Godfather Part II*)? They might start out as assholes, but they usually end up as something else. And even when they start out, there's something we like about them—their sense of humor, their looks, their vulnerability (again, think of the Jim Carrey character in *Liar Liar*). And, importantly, their flaws and quirks. Flaws make a character more interesting. Even the good guy has some bad qualities. Part of the conflict is in fighting those qualities.

If it's the antagonist we're talking about—the villain—then a whole flip side of questions must be asked. Why do we hate this character? Why do we want this character to lose? Why do they stir some emotion in us? And what's this character like when they are at home with their family? What's their good side? Because even the bad guy has some good qualities. Something very human.

THE MIDPOINT

One of the most difficult to write, yet one of the most crucial, points of your film is the midpoint or turning point. Yes, this *does* happen right around the middle, wherein the action takes a sudden and unexpected direction. The goal may change. The central character may realize what their flaw is. Their true needs become more important than what they want.

We've discussed this before, in detail, but it's worth returning to. In *Thelma & Louise,* Jimmy, Louise's boyfriend, is waiting for Louise at the hotel where he was supposed to wire her the money. She gives the money to Thelma for safekeeping, and we should know by now that something's going to go wrong with that, but we don't. After J.D. (Brad Pitt) steals the money, Thelma stops being pulled along by events. She takes charge. The action spins off in a new and unexpected direction: The women go on a crime spree!

Just before the middle of *In & Out*, Howard, played by Kevin Kline, is still determined to prove that he is not gay. In a masterpiece visual, he literally bumps into the one person who can help him, not coincidentally at a crossroads.

The catalyst for his self-discovery is Peter Malloy, played by Tom Selleck, an out-of-the-closet journalist who just won't let the story go. He forces Howard to come to terms with himself. How? By knocking him over at an intersection—literally the crossroads of his life. By kissing him full on the mouth and making him accept the fact that he likes it.

Now Howard's task is to come to grips with the fact that he's gay. The story spins off in a different direction. His goal is different.

In *Unforgiven*, the midpoint comes when Will (Clint Eastwood), Ned (Morgan Freeman), and the Kid ambush the cowboys, and Will, missing a few times, finally kills one of them. But the experience reminds Ned why he gave up gunslinging, and he pulls out of the deal.

Lots has happened up to this point in *Unforgiven*, most of which has been setup for things to come. The only obstacle has been the confrontation in the billiard house, but it really hasn't stopped them from reaching at least part of their goal. But now that Will is without his partner, he's left with an untried, unpredictable kid. Things are going to be different.

This is the midpoint, the turning point of the film. Things are going in a new direction now for two reasons: Ned's gone, and Little Bill forms a posse to find who killed the cowboys. These actions lead to deputies finding Ned on the trail and bringing him in, while the Kid and Will sneak up on the ranch. It also sets in motion events that will return, in part, the story to more traditional themes. It changes Will's goal. Now he must rescue Ned or, failing that, avenge him.

The midpoint, or turning point as it's sometimes called, is often neglected by new writers because it requires going deep into the character and finding out what they really *need*, then expressing this new goal in those terms. It also frequently means a new awareness by the protagonist of their own flaws and a desire to remedy them. A tough sequence to write, but once written, it can really make your whole film.

Assignment

1. Write ten new pages in your screenplay. Now the story is driven by the new goal—what the protagonist needs. Is it clear? Is it more important than what they wanted? Are they working toward that new goal? Did they abandon the old goal, or is it still worth pursuing?
2. In your writers group, talk about how your scripts have changed direction. Is the new goal a worthy goal? Are there enough barriers to that goal?

Lesson Four

ESCALATING CONFLICT

If you have the biggest, baddest, toughest scene in the first act, where do you go from there? Why would anyone want to continue to watch?

A good screenwriter *builds* the conflict. Each barrier facing the protagonist on their way to their goal gets a little tougher, a little more difficult, until the final challenge presents a barrier that seems impossible, that will require your protagonist to exert themself more than they ever have before, that will, in fact, require them to go above and beyond their capabilities in order to prevail.

You save the best for last.

Everything is aiming toward this point, which is why it's a good idea to think of this point, the final challenge, before you even start writing the first word of the script. Yes, I know, some people would disagree, but not many. You must know where you're going in order to get there, or you could end up someplace that doesn't make sense.

THE GOAL

The driving force of every story is the protagonist's wants and needs, which compel them to create first one goal, then another. And what's behind this drive is their flaw, which creates the need for change.

Let's explore once again the seven points in the three-act structure that most scripts use as their foundation and relate them to the goal so that there is no misunderstanding about the importance of knowing your character's goal.

1. **Ordinary Life:** getting to know who the central character is and what their issue is. We see their flaw and how they need to change because of it. This creates the need for a goal because the change will only come about in pursuit of the goal.
2. **Inciting Incident:** usually around page fifteen, give or take a couple of pages. This is what changes their life forever. This compels them to act. This compels them to search for an appropriate goal, one that will change their life, one that will fix the situation created by the inciting incident.
3. **End of Act I:** when something happens that compels your character to decide on a goal and a course of action (a plan) in order to deal with whatever the inciting incident brought up. So the goal is set, and your protagonist must pursue this goal throughout the first half of act II. If they don't, the story doesn't move.
4. **Midpoint or Turning Point:** when the goal may change. The central character may realize what their flaw is. The want becomes a need. For example, the protagonist may realize they're a nymphomaniac because their father abandoned them at an early age. They stop pursuing a man and start looking to create a family because that's what they really need. The second part of act II is about the pursuit of that goal.
5. **Low Point:** end of the second act. The all is lost point in terms of the goal. There seems to be no way in hell they'll ever reach their goal. It doesn't matter that their Aunt Matilda has died, it doesn't matter that they've lost an arm, it doesn't matter that their cat ran away—all sad things. The only thing that matters here is that it appears that they won't reach their goal, the one that was set at

the midpoint. Also, their emotional relationship must appear to be out of reach.

6. **Final Challenge:** that final test, the final barrier that your character must overcome in order to reach their goal. Very close to the end. And they must reach it, even if they die in the process, as did the Gladiator in his final challenge. At least in an American film, the protagonist must win, which is not necessarily the same thing as a happy ending.
7. **Return to (the Forever Changed) Normal Life:** two or three pages to show us that life goes on and that our character has triumphed. They can enjoy the rewards of reaching their goal.

It's all about the goal.

Let me say that again.

It's all about the goal.

THE ANTAGONIST

If there is no barrier for your protagonist, they will achieve their goal immediately. There is no conflict, so there is no story. (Remember the definition of story?) While this may occasionally happen in real life, it is rare that someone achieves a goal without some difficulty. The more difficulty, the sweeter the victory, and the more interesting a story to tell.

The same applies to movie life. If there is nothing to overcome, there is no story. The movie's over before it has a chance to start. So there must be something or someone in opposition, something or someone that makes it hard, almost impossible, for your protagonist to reach their goal. Without struggle there is no story, and the bigger the struggle, the better the story.

So your protagonist must have opposition. And the clearest way to put roadblocks in front of your central character is to have another person be in the way. There are some exceptions—nature is antagonist enough for *The Perfect Storm* or *Volcano.* In a war movie, it's the enemy, sometimes personified but often not.

What is an antagonist? It's a person whose goals are in conflict with the protagonist. It could be a business competitor, a competitor in love, a criminal (if your protagonist is a detective), a detective (if your protagonist is a criminal), anyone who has a reason to be in the way of the protagonist's goal and actively exercises it.

The antagonist is the second-most important person in your film. They have to be a worthy opponent because they must provide the most important barrier to the protagonist's drive toward their goal. If they are too weak, then the fight is too small. They must be stronger than the protagonist, better, faster, smarter, more handsome (in a romantic comedy, at least). Their opposition must force the protagonist to rise above themself to reach their goal. They must be a worthy foe. If they're not, there is no movie.

ADDING DEPTH

If your antagonist is a human being, they must have human qualities to avoid being two-dimensional and predictable. A purely evil protagonist is not interesting. Even a man who runs a concentration camp, exterminating people all day long, may return to a loving wife, children, and dog (as in *The Zone of Interest*). A murderer may have a weakness for sweets. A business rival may harbor a secret passion for music—or S&M. This adds depth to the characterization as well as reality. Even Hitler was reputedly kind to his secretary, and there is footage of him playing with his dogs. It makes his evil all the more chilling.

Just as your protagonist must have a flaw, your antagonist must have a good quality, one the audience can identify as human.

I'm not saying, either, that your antagonist has to be evil. In a romantic comedy, they shouldn't be. They should be a serious possibility when it comes to being a possible love object for one of the characters (see *Tin Cup* or *His Girl Friday*). In a sports movie, they're the opposition, though often less morally worthy of the goal than the protagonist, but they are not pure evil (*Bad News Bears*, *Rocky*). That's too easy. Yes, we still must have a reason to consider them less worthy of winning, so they must have some evil characteristics. But they are a human being, with all the wants and needs of a human being.

How do you draw a character like this? The same way you develop the protagonist. So, ask yourself, do you know this character as well as you know your protagonist?

Also, be careful to include a humanizing trait. Nobody is completely evil. Nobody is completely good. To be believable, your antagonist must ring true as a person.

REVEALING YOUR ANTAGONIST

Character is action. Action is character. As you write, look for places to show how the antagonist interacts with people on a daily basis, how they interact with their confederates or their family. Look for places to show their human side. And, especially, look for places to show their strengths and weaknesses, and, if necessary, their evil.

Just as the protagonist has a voice, so should the antagonist, assuming your antagonist is a person. Things to check for in the antagonist's dialogue: Are they too arch (over-the-top evil)? Do they sound human, or are they just a writer's two-dimensional conceit to move the story along?

Make sure the protagonist and the antagonist are not speaking with the same voice. Their rhythms of speech should be distinct. Their vocabularies in contrast. Ensure that how they say something is as important as what they say.

For an excellent example of contrasting manners of speech, and a worthy opponent, look at Hans Gruber, the character played by Alan Rickman in *Die Hard*. Here is an antagonist whose speech demonstrates his erudition and ruthlessness. He is able, in a critical moment, to imitate the speech of an American executive, thus showing his cunning. His manner of talking is a fundamental element of his character, just as fundamental as John McClane's (Bruce Willis) blue collar, wise cracking, no-nonsense speech.

But it isn't only his speech that he uses to deceive McClane, it is his cowering manner. He "acts" the victim to perfection, trying to gain McClane's confidence. Eventually, McClane gives him a pistol. Once he has his hands on the pistol, his whole demeanor changes, and he becomes Hans again. There's another reversal when he discovers the pistol is not loaded and that he hasn't fooled McClane after all. And yet another reversal when other members of his gang burst out of the elevator.

Definitely a worthy foe—ruthless, cunning, quick-witted, multilingual. Try and stop him!

McClane finally does, but he pays a price. It isn't easy, but the journey is worth it.

Assignment

1. Write ten new pages in your screenplay.
2. Review the midpoint to make sure there is a change in direction.
3. Are you halfway through writing your script based on your treatment? Check to see how pages of treatment correspond to script pages.
4. Review how you've written your antagonist. Are they a real person? Do they have flaws and strengths? Are they a worthy opponent?
5. In your writers group, discuss outstanding antagonists in movies that you've seen.

Lesson Five

SETUPS AND PAYOFFS

This is just as simple as it sounds. Partly, it's your responsibility as a writer to make sure that everything in your story is there for a reason. Things can't just come from nowhere; they must be set up. If the protagonist of the film suddenly grabs a rifle and picks off a sniper, you have to set up earlier in the story that they are a super marksman. If your romantic interest knows the name of your protagonist in their first meeting, you have to set up that they've seen their picture in the newspaper.

Similarly, if you show the character putting a gun in their purse, you must pay it off, as in *Thelma & Louise.* If you show your character getting a lesson in going barefoot, you must pay it off, as they do in *Die Hard.*

Assignment

1. Review the first half of your script to make sure you've set up everything you pay off in the second half. Also make sure you pay off every setup.
2. Write ten new pages in your screenplay.
3. In your writers group, read your latest pages out loud. Do the protagonist and antagonist have distinct voices? Does the dialogue sound natural?

Lesson Six

TO THE BONE

Screenwriting is the art of saying a lot with very few words. Given the more than fifty thousand screenplays, treatments, and teleplays registered with the Writers Guild every year, it's not hard to imagine that readers (meaning people hired to read screenplays—development executives, agents, and producers) want a quick read. They want to get to the good stuff as soon as possible. So you have to make your screenplay as lean as possible.

Another reason it has to be lean is that it will seem more exciting that way. Shorter, faster description sweeps the reader up better than long, drawn-out description of extraneous details. Action requires action writing.

Every first draft I've ever seen could be improved by simply taking 10 percent off (just like the purchase price of a car is improved). How can you do that without skimping on your story?

THE FIRST STEP TO PAGE REDUCTION

Cut out all fat. Sounds like the latest diet from South Beach, but no, it's the rule that you must eliminate anything that doesn't move the story forward. Does every single scene move the story forward or reveal something crucial about your protagonist? Preferably, each scene does both. If not, try to combine some scenes. If a scene does neither, cut it. Be ruthless. If you're not sure, take the scene out for a moment, then read what was the scene before and what was the scene after, without the scene in question. Do you lose anything? Does the story still make sense? If the first answer is no and the second is yes, then leave that scene out. If you can get by with just a little additional work in the preceding or following scene, then do that. If there's no way in hell your movie can move forward without that scene, then leave it in.

CUTTING DOWN SCENES

But it may not be enough to cut scenes. You may have to trim each individual scene. There's one easy way—cut out as much of the head and tail of the scene as you can. In other words, enter late and leave early. You may be able to take out ten percent of your scene this way, and that would be good. If the ordinary life of the scene can be inferred by the reader, and if the return to ordinary life can be inferred as well, you've got some easy cuts. But if that's not enough . . .

Cut down on description, especially specifics as to the decoration of a room, the foliage of an outdoor place, or whatever gets in the way of the forward action. Certainly, take out any camera direction and placement. That's not for you to determine anyway, and it only gets in the way of the reading. Let the director and cinematographer do their jobs. All you want to do is to enable the reader to visualize the story, not every single shot.

CUTTING DIALOGUE

Now it's time to attack the dialogue. First, make sure that you must absolutely have to have that information in dialogue. It's probably more effective to see in action: Action is quicker. They're called *motion* pictures, and if you can move your story forward with moving pictures only, you'll make more of an impression on your audience than if you rely entirely on words (dialogue). If you illuminate your character through a physical attribute or something they do, it's always going to be better than having you tell about it in dialogue.

Then, assuming you've changed any dialogue to action that you could, are all the remaining words necessary? Quite often, you'll find that characters go through a little "throat clearing" at the beginning of their speeches. Sometimes, that can be good as a specific trait of your character. But mostly it's not. It's a waste of readers' time, just like "Hello. How are you?" would be. Or even a "goodbye" on the telephone. If they waste time, if they're not absolutely needed, then they're out.

Then there's dialogue that's unnecessary because you've already told the reader or the audience that information in another way. Often, you'll have one character tell another character something they don't know but that the reader knows because they've read it earlier. In that case, cut deeper into the scene. Sometimes you'll write something in description that a character then describes in dialogue. Cut one or the other. Preferably the dialogue.

Ten percent doesn't look like such a difficult target anymore, does it?

Assignment

1. Take your ten best pages of your screenplay and make them into eight without changing margins. Cut description or dialogue—whatever you can without harming the story.
2. Write five new pages.
3. In your writers group, read out loud a scene that needs cutting. Ask your colleagues what could be cut.

Lesson Seven

HOW LOW CAN YOU GO?

You already know that each story point has meaning in reference to the goal (see page 173 if you've forgotten). Yes, the goal may change (and should) at the midpoint, but story points following that will be in relation to the new goal. That means the low point is the low in terms of (not) achieving that new goal. It also should be the low in terms of the central emotional relationship. In other words, everything looks bad for our protagonist at that point. This is why Lew Hunter, the former head of UCLA's screenwriting department, called it "the big gloom."

But one thing many people forget is that the low should be caused by the protagonist themself. Usually, that means their flaw has somehow screwed things up: They were too impetuous, too shy, too selfish, too weak, too overbearing. Whatever their flaw is, you can bet it will come into play in determining how they got into the low point.

Let's take another look at *Thelma & Louise.* Thelma's goal by the midpoint of the film is to find out who she really is and to get to Mexico. When she and Louise call Darryl after robbing a convenience store and performing other questionable acts, Louise asks him to put the cops on, and Hal takes the phone. He wants them to turn themselves him, and he knows they're going to Mexico.

This is the low point of the film, the end of the second act. Nothing's going well. And now the cops know where they're headed. It's the one thing they had going for them—the cops didn't know they were going to Mexico. It causes a rift between Thelma and Louise, but they pull together. They're frightened but determined. They head off into the night.

In the original *Star Wars*, George Lucas uses another structure that works well for adventure films—the mythic structure. This twelve-point structure has added story points, but the film can be analyzed just as accurately using the three-act, seven-point paradigm. In this case, the goal is to escape the Death Star and warn the rebels that the Empire is coming to get them. There, Luke is pulled under water by the garbage monster, and all appears to be lost; but, as if that's not enough, the walls move in to crush Luke and his team. It looks like they're never going to get out.

Again, your protagonist must appear to have lost everything.

Just so we comply with the rule of three, let's discuss *The Wizard of Oz*. The midpoint goal is to capture the witch's broom and return with it to Oz so they can go home, but before Dorothy and her cohorts reach their new goal, the flying monkeys find them, and Dorothy reaches the low point in her journey in relation to the goal. There appears no way now that she'll ever return home.

But that's not all that has to happen around this point in your script. Somehow, after this complete devastation, your protagonist must rise up and renew their quest for the goal. How does that happen? Nine out of ten times, something has to happen to them, somebody has got to talk to them, they've got to see something from the outside that reanimates them and makes them find something deep inside of themself in order to prepare for the final challenge that lies ahead. This is really the beginning of the third act and sets up the action that is now going to take place. This is the rising action, where your protagonist must get ready to face the biggest barrier between them and their goal.

What must your character be doing now? Recovering from the hit they took at the low point. Learning more about the enemy. Planning.

Training. Making sure the team is ready. Whatever it takes to get ready to meet the antagonist head-on.

Does this apply to a romantic comedy, too? Glad you asked.

In a romantic comedy, the "A" story, the central story, is the relationship story. So the central character and the love interest have to be completely on the outs at the end of act II, and it has to be the central character's fault. Again, it has to be something she has said or done that reveals her flaw sneaking back into her personality. And she has to believe that there's no way she's going to get the guy no matter what she does.

But then . . . something comes along to remind her why she loves this guy so danged much and why she's willing to sacrifice everything to win him back. Maybe it's her best friend telling her this is her last chance for happiness. Maybe it's her kid telling her he knows a way to get back into the good graces of the guy who's been his stand-in father. Whatever it is, now she's got to think of a way to make up for her mistake and go get the guy, whether that requires walking across Manhattan on her knees or singing "Love Will Keep Us Together" a cappella at his corporate dinner.

It's going to be up to her to win him back, and she's going to have to figure out how to do it.

So, has your protagonist faced their low point? What will bring them out of it?

Assignment

1. Have a close look at your low point. Is it low in terms of the midpoint goal, or is it just that someone has died (which may be important, but not necessarily)?
2. Write ten new pages in your screenplay.
3. In your writers group, discuss your low point pages. Do they make the reader believe there is no way the protagonist is going to reach their goal?

Lesson Eight

THE FINAL CHALLENGE

Most people call this part of your movie the climax, and there's nothing wrong with calling it that. But in my mind, it's not a very active term for what must be the most active scene or sequence in the entire movie.

By this point in your movie, your protagonist knows what they must face to achieve their goal. They know what they have to overcome inside themself in order to prevail against the forces outside themself, and they're ready to do that. They're prepared, maybe not as much as they would like, but there's no going back now. They have too much to lose, the stakes are too high (and they'd better be) for them to say "Never mind."

But sometimes the protagonist and the audience are fooled. They think they've faced their foe and won, only to be challenged by a force even stronger than the last. This is a standard false ending often used in horror pictures. It even crashed its way into *Fatal Attraction*. It works in certain kinds of films best—thrillers and horror pictures, not so well in romantic comedies or teen coming-of-age flicks. I don't recommend using it unless you're writing the kind of movie in which the audience expects to see it. I'm not saying it wouldn't work for your movie, just that it may be hard to pull off.

THE REAL FINAL CHALLENGE

The last barrier between the protagonist and their true goal must be formidable. It must be the toughest thing your character has had to face. They must bring everything they've learned during the course of the film to bear, which means they must face the last barrier themself. Not by themself, but they must be the single most important person in its defeat. Sure, there can be help—a team, a support system—but the protagonist must be the agent of their own salvation. They can't be saved by anyone else. The cavalry cannot come in at the last minute and save them, although that has happened in some films. Not satisfying.

YOUR SCHEDULE

You should be close to writing the final challenge, but if you aren't, you probably know the answer why not. There are three things that interfere with a writing schedule.

Whoops, wait a minute, you say you don't have a writing schedule?

Okay, there are four things that interfere with a writing schedule—the first one is not having one. With all the pressures of your life, if you don't set aside a specific time and amount of time to write each day (five out of seven will do), you are not going to be able to do what you want to do—namely, write and rewrite a complete filmscript in the time it would take to complete this course. If, on the other hand, you're not in a hurry and have years in which to complete the task, well then, take your time and write when the spirit moves you, the kids are at Grandma's, and the boss has given you a bonus day off.

Otherwise, welcome to the club. If you're a night owl, tag an hour a day onto your schedule or reduce what you need to do in favor of what you want to do. If you write better in the morning (and most people do, even though they object to the time), get up an hour early, preferably before the kids, pets, or significant others are up. There's peace then, and you'll need it. You may have to go to bed before *The Daily Show* comes on, but we all have to make sacrifices.

A ROOM OF YOUR OWN

It helps to have a specific place, too, so you don't have to go through a warm-up each time to get started (you know, setting up the computer, making space, setting out your pens, whatever). Okay, it can be Starbucks or the library, as long as you can focus there, but it must be a place where you won't be disturbed. Failing that, it's a place and time when those who have demands on your time recognize that you're busy and are not to be disturbed. With small children and significant others of all ages, this requires some training, because you may not look busy. But we know you are, even if you're playing computer solitaire. Sometimes your brain needs recess, just like in elementary school.

Can you spare an hour a day to do this? Or maybe all day Sunday, or half a day Saturday and half a day Sunday. Whatever you decide, try to set a target in terms of pages and always meet it, no matter what. Forget about quality for the moment. As a matter of fact, *set out* to write a certain number of *bad* pages per session. That way, it'll be harder to fail. What's easier to do, write one perfect page or two bad pages per day? First drafts are *supposed* to be bad, so worry about quality in the next draft. For now, just get words down on paper; then you have something to work with.

Two bad pages per day times five days per week is one hundred pages in the course of a ten-week class. More than enough. How about eight bad pages per weekend? You're there!

Either way, you have less pressure if you just write and don't judge along the way. That's not to say, however, that I don't want you to take ten minutes to proofread those pages before you have someone read them. Please do. The small things drive readers nuts and distract us from what's really important—your story.

THE THREE THINGS

By the way, the three things that interfere with your writing schedule: your work, your relationships, and fatigue. How you deal with them will decide if you can do this.

Assignment

1. Fine-tune your schedule. Is it working for you? How could you make it better?
2. Write ten pages of your screenplay. You should be near the end.
3. In your writers group, read five pages aloud. Do you notice a difference from earlier pages?

Lesson Nine

THE PUKE DRAFT REVISITED

You remember what a puke draft is, right? It's the one that flows out willy-nilly, sometimes formless, raw, spontaneous. It's the purest form, undisturbed by your own censor or anyone else's comments. It's the way you should write the first draft of your screenplay and anything else you write.

But as if that's not hard enough to do, once you're done with that draft, you've got to start the rewrite process. Here's where the craft comes in, where you analyze the dialogue, weight the acts, follow the plotlines, and check for sense and continuity. This requires reviewing your screenplay in a number of "passes"—poring over your screenplay carefully.

THE EIGHT PASSES

Pass 1: The first thing you're going to do is read for structure. Make sure your seven points are fully realized and balanced in terms of page length. Make sure your scenes have a beginning, middle, and end.

Pass 2: Next, make sure the scenes have conflict and that they move the story forward. Cut any scenes that don't.

Pass 3: Now, read your descriptive paragraphs again. Are they terse? Do they move the story? Do they tell the story in images? Are they grammatically correct when they need to be?

Pass 4: There are three separate reads for dialogue. In each, you should ask yourself if you can show it rather than say it. In other words, could your characters be doing something instead of talking about it? Then you'll ask if each word—I mean each *a* and *the*—is necessary. The first dialogue pass is for the main character. Read each of their speeches, and only their speeches. Are they consistent in voice? Could another character have said those words? Does their voice stand out from the crowd?

Pass 5: Do the same for the antagonist.

Pass 6: Do the same for supporting characters.

Pass 7: Go over the whole script one more time and look for cuts. Look for couplets (dialogue pairs—one person talks, another responds, once each) that repeat parts of the conversation, lack conflict, or, in the case of a comedy, just aren't funny. Then cut them. Delete any nonessential scenes; cut off heads and tails of scenes, if possible; cut down dialogue. Yes, again.

Pass 8: Lastly, do the final spelling, punctuation, grammar, and sense pass. I call this the Mercedes pass. Why? Because when you're hired to write a screenplay, your pay is roughly equivalent to the cost of a new Mercedes-Benz S 580 (once taxes, destination charges, etc., are added). But consider this. If you go into a Mercedes showroom and there are two identical S 580s on the floor, and one is in pristine condition, has that new car smell, and you can see yourself in the shiny black paint job, while the other one is missing a hubcap, the screen on the dashboard is mounted cock-eyed, the steering wheel leather covering is torn, and the seats are slashed, which one are you going to pay six figures for? Same applies to the screenplay that hasn't been properly prepared for sale.

By the way, you should do this for each draft.

WHO'S GOING TO READ IT NOW?

When you think the dialogue is lean and mean and the description leaps from the pages, when you've poured everything into them, then share them once again with your writers group. They're going to have something to say about them, just as they would if Christopher Nolan, Greta Gerwig, or Eric Roth shared their pages. We all need feedback. In the environment of a writers group, it's nonthreatening. In the real world, try to find someone whose opinions you respect to read and give you notes in the same way. Do the same for them. Only after you've gone through a couple of drafts with your trusted advisor (whom you might recruit from among your writers group) should you show your script to an agent or producer.

Assignment

1. Write ten pages of your screenplay. You should be near the end. If you're not, get there.
2. In your writers group, read the final challenge scene aloud. Is it thrilling? Gripping? Funny? Satisfying?

Lesson Ten

THE LOGLINE, THE PARAGRAPH, AND THE LEAVE-BEHIND

You've probably heard people ask for the logline of your film. What they're referring to is the logline in the *TV Guide* (remember that magazine? No? Too bad. It used to be a staple for every household) or the newspaper that sums up your story in one simple line: A cop on the verge of divorce has to overcome his fear of heights to save his wife from international thieves who are not afraid to kill. That would be the logline for the original *Die Hard*. What you may notice about it is that it sums up John McClane's inner flaw, his relationship, and the external storyline, all in just a few words. This is what you must do with your story, too.

If, when you tell someone your logline, they want to hear more, be prepared with a paragraph that covers the beginning, middle, and end. By *ready with a paragraph*, I mean write it and memorize it, though make it sound like you've just seen the most exciting movie in the world and you're describing it to a friend.

If you're lucky, after your pitch is over (during which you will tell your story's seven points, describe the main characters, and be enthusiastic), an executive may ask you to leave a few pages behind, which they'll call a "leave-behind." They're not supposed to, but they often do—which is to your benefit. In those pages you will again present the story in its briefest form, writing the seven story points with descriptions in under two pages. Executives use these to keep track of pitches and to "pitch it up" to the next level. Never rely on their notes to tell your story. Always leave something. Though the guild frowns on this practice, I would rather have the executive use your leave-behind than rely on their notes about the pitch.

These days they might even ask if you have a pitch deck. In other words, have you worked out casting suggestions, production design, even music in a PowerPoint or similar presentation? It truly is wrong that you have to do half the preproduction for them, but, and I hate to say it, it does help to sell a project. They're not supposed to ask for a presentation, either, but you can surely offer it. Again, the Writers Guild hates this, as it's basically writing for free, but if you're pitching an already written script, give yourself the best chance for selling it you can.

Postscript

WAX ON, WAX OFF

The words of Mr. Miyagi (played by Pat Morita) to Daniel LaRusso (Ralph Macchio), his student, in *The Karate Kid,* are meant to point out that the movements used in washing and waxing his car are the foundational movements he will use in the practice of karate. Those words, written by Robert Mark Kamen, are a good reminder that what you've gleaned from these pages is meant to be the foundational principles of screenwriting, and it's up to you to apply them as you see fit in whatever way supports your writing. You may find other ways of doing things, and I encourage that. But you can always count on wax on, wax off.

Before I send you out to the cruel world that is the business of show, let's go over a few things you need to keep in mind as you reread what you've written so far (and you're going to read it what seems like a billion times before it's in theaters or on streamers).

If I were to give you a final exam, here are the questions I would ask. And maybe some of the answers.

Do you know the definition of story? Of course you do. There's a person with a goal. There's a barrier to reaching that goal. The person has to go over, under, around, or through the barrier to get to the goal.

So, you need to know who the person is. And you need to know the other people the person interacts with, so you need to write character descriptions that include the physiology, sociology, and psychology of these people. And you have to match them to your premise.

What is your premise? What are you trying to say with your story? Why are you even writing this, in addition to wanting to entertain an audience and earn a living?

Once you set your characters in motion, do you have the structure that will help you tell your story? Remember the seven points of the three-act structure of nearly every film that's come out of Hollywood: The ordinary life of the protagonist. The inciting incident. The end of act I goal and plan. The midpoint (turning point), where there's a change of direction. The low point end of act II. The final challenge (climax). And the return to normal life.

Did you beat out your story to fill in the spaces between these points? Does each scene have seven points, whether stated or implied? Does each sequence have seven points? Structure is expected and necessary for readers and audiences to be able to follow your story.

Maybe you've decided to use the mythic structure instead of the traditional seven-point, three-act structure. Great! You probably will still see the seven points on top of that, as you can with *The Wizard of Oz*. Of course, if you have written a love story, the mythic structure might not be the best way to go. If you've written a space opera, however, mythic twelve-point structure seems natural.

I know you've focused on the main story, but have you developed the story of the central emotional relationship, too? People go to movies to experience emotions, and to do that, they need to see people having emotions. And the emotions relating to the central emotional relationship are key to having a compelling script.

There are lots of other characters to think about. Do they have interesting traits? Are they characters to remember?

Is what those characters say unique to their personalities? Is it appropriate to the location and situation? Characters' dialogue should reflect their goals, their backgrounds, their state of mind, their status in the scene, and even their location.

Speaking of goals, as you review your script, be sure to check that there are barriers to those goals in every scene. In other words, there is *conflict* in every scene.

And the scene itself should have one of two goals: either to move the story forward or to illuminate the character. If the scene doesn't do either one of those things, you don't need that scene.

And in each scene, do the actions of your characters tell the story or do you rely on their dialogue? Action is character, so you can say a lot by making your characters active. Showing is better than telling. (I know you've heard that a million times, but just in case . . .)

Of course, you're writing those actions in your descriptions. And your descriptions are succinct, the paragraphs are short, and your pages have lots of white space so they're easy to read. Right?

As a matter of fact, before you can say you've finished a "puke draft," you might want to read over the whole script and make cuts where you can. Have you said something in dialogue that you already have shown in description? Can you cut the dialogue by, say, ten percent? Are there scenes that don't have conflict? Are there scenes that don't move the story or tell something new about the central character? Did you do the eight passes? Did rereading your script make you laugh, cringe, or cry? I hope so. If it didn't, go back and make it bring out some emotion. And even if it did, get ready for the next draft.

WHAT'S IT WORTH NOW?

Through these courses, you may have created a document worth hundreds of thousands of dollars or about two cents in recycled paper. Some of that is up to me, much of it is up to you, but much of it is up to luck and the fickle market. At this stage in your careers, though, it's not realistic to assume you're going to sell it to anyone until it's been converted into a fully realized script (meaning one that's been rewritten about twenty-five times). Good luck. I know you can do it.

Assignment

1. Celebrate having written a full-length screenplay. You didn't finish? Then finish. (And then celebrate.)
2. Put your puke draft in a drawer (metaphorically speaking) for at least two weeks.
3. Share your screenplay with two or three trusted advisors (from your writers group, if possible). Ask them to tell you the truth. Listen to what they say. Take from them what helps your screenplay. Whatever advice doesn't help your vision, just say, "Thanks for that. I'll look into it."
4. Make a plan to rewrite your first draft. A good place to start is to look at my book *Rewrite: A Step-by-Step Guide to Strengthen Structure, Characters, and Drama in Your Screenplay, 2nd Edition.* Oh, you say, I mentioned that earlier? Then you already have it, right? If not, get it at the library.
5. Follow the rewrite plan.

See you at the guild.

GLOSSARY

act (noun): a division of a screenplay. Most screenplays have three acts; some have five.

act (verb): to perform a part in a film or stage play

antagonist: the force acting against the protagonist. Could be a person or an act of nature, a government, an army, etc.

art director: the person responsible for the look of the set

beat: a moment, a pause. Sometimes refers to a whole scene.

beat sheet: a collection of the beats or scenes in the film with minimal descriptions

character arc: the journey of self-discovery and change a character undergoes

cinematographer: the person in charge of the camera and lighting

climax: the final challenge; the biggest scene of conflict in the film

coverage: 1) a written review of the script; 2) the series of shots from various angles in a film

development executive: a person from a studio or production company who helps choose and then guides a film project

DP: director of photography; cinematographer

filmscript: the written guide of the movie, containing dialogue and descriptions of locations and actions

final challenge: climax; the biggest scene of the movie in terms of action and conflict

foreshadowing: hinting at what is to come

INT., EXT.: Interior, Exterior; parts of the scene headings delineating whether the action is indoors or outdoors

inciting incident: the occurrence that triggers the action of a story

intercut: the editing technique of cutting back and forth between different locations

midpoint: the turning point of the film for the protagonist

mythic structure: a twelve-point film structure based on storytelling originally described by Joseph Campbell and often used in quest and action films

notes: suggestions or comments that a development executive, agent, manager, director, or producer gives in written or oral form about a script or another aspect of the filmmaking process

outline: a term used loosely by some in the film industry to mean a written document of the basic bones of a script. The term is not recognized by the Writers Guild of America.

O.S.: off-screen; used to denote dialogue or sound from something that can't be seen in the visual frame but is generally in the same location

pass: To "give it a pass" can mean 1) rejecting the project, or 2) revising the script one more time.

parenthetical expression: a direction for the actor just under their character's name in the script, before their dialogue. Mainly used to indicate emotions not evident in dialogue.

plot point: a description of an important moment or group of moments of the film. Some films have seven points; others have twelve.

plotline: the progress of the story

polish: a minor revision of the script, usually near the end of the writing process

POV: point of view

premise: the overall theme of the film; sometimes the driving concept

production designer: the person who designs the look of the film

production manager: the person who organizes the physical production of the film

props person, property manager: the person who finds and then places items to be used by actors in the film

protagonist: the central character of a film

scene: a self-contained moment in a film that has its own beginning, middle, and end

scene heading: a line at the beginning of a scene in the script that indicates time and place

screenplay: the written blueprint of a film containing dialogue and descriptions of locations and actions

script: screenplay

sequence: a group of scenes with a particular collective theme or intent

set: where the action of a film is staged, whether indoors or outdoors

slugline: scene heading

socko: adjective describing something that is especially effective or successful

sotto: short for sotto voce, Italian for *whisper*

split screen: a film screen that is divided into two or more parts

story: The Writers Guild's term for a prose description of everything in the movie; also a description of the action of a film: A person has a goal. They confront barriers to reaching that goal. They go over, under, around, or through those barriers.

> **"A" story:** the protagonist's main story
>
> **"B" story:** the protagonist's story regarding their central emotional relationship
>
> **"C" story:** the protagonist's story regarding their personal development

subplot: the "B" or "C" stories or another story involving supporting characters

subtext: the underlying meaning of an exchange of dialogue

treatment: The Writers Guild of America's term for a film story; see *story*

UPM: Unit Production Manager; see *production manager*

V.O.: voice over; a voice that is not in or even outside the frame, heard by the audience but usually not the actors in the scene

WGA: the Writers Guild of America, the union of screen, video game, and radio writers

WGA Schedule of Minimums: the contracted minimum rates of pay agreed upon by the WGA and the Motion Picture Association (the organization of the major studios and production companies)

writers room: on a television show, the room where the writers discuss the stories and scripts for the show

ACKNOWLEDGMENTS

The idea for this book grew out of a suggestion by Jody Wheeler, whose continued support buoys me in a stormy world. My thanks go to my publishers—Geraldine Overton-Wiese, Ken Lee, and Alexander Ward—for their faith in me and their dedication to educating future filmmakers. I also want to thank Linda Venus, the former head of the writing program at UCLA Extension, who helped make the Extension the everyman's film school. Many thanks go to Jim Schmerer, RIP, of the UCLA Professional Program in Screenwriting for his valuable insights on movies and teaching. I always told my students to call me whatever they wanted, so I thank Emiliano Flores, probably the first student to call me sensei. Thanks to other students who called me professor, profe, Dr. Chitlik, Paul, and "hey you." Thanks to Karen Krumpak, my stalwart copy editor, who flagged a significant number of errors in the manuscript and guided me toward better clarity. Any bad writing or punctuation still left in this book is due to my hardheadedness. Thanks to Bill Morosi for his stunning book design. My thanks to John Brenner for his kickass cover. I shared it with great pride months before publication. And my eternal thanks to my wife, Beth McCauley, who encourages me, tolerates me, and loves me.

ABOUT THE AUTHOR

Paul Chitlik has written for all the major networks and studios in English and in Spanish. He was story editor for MGM/UA's 1985 reboot of *The Twilight Zone* and staff writer for Showtime's sitcom *Brothers*.

Paul has written features for Rysher Entertainment, NuImage, Promark, Mainline Releasing, and others. He has directed episodes and been coordinating producer for *Real Stories of the Highway Patrol* and *U.S. Customs Classified*. He wrote and produced *Alien Abduction*, the first network movie shot on digital video for UPN. He wrote, produced, and directed *Ringling Brothers Revealed*, a special for the Travel Channel. (He had been a roustabout for Circus Vargas years earlier.) Most recently he wrote, produced, and directed *The Wedding Dress* for Amazon Prime. He received a Writers Guild of America award nomination for his work on *The Twilight Zone* and a GLAAD Media Award nomination for *Los Beltrán*, a Telemundo show. He won a Genesis Award for a Showtime Family movie.

He has taught in the MFA programs of UCLA, the University of Barcelona's film school ESCAC, Cuba's film school EICTV, Chile's film school UNIACC, the University of Zulia in Venezuela, the Panamerican University in Mexico City, the Story Academy of Sweden, and as a clinical associate professor at Loyola Marymount University. Paul is now writing full-time again and living near his grandson in Chapel

Hill, NC, with his wife, television producer Beth McCauley. His book *Rewrite* is used in film schools around the world (in English, Chinese, and Korean). His latest novel is *Lies, All Lies*.

Learn more at his website: PaulChitlik.com.

REWRITE:

2ND EDITION

A STEP-BY-STEP GUIDE TO STRENGTHEN STRUCTURE, CHARACTERS, AND DRAMA IN YOUR SCREENPLAY

PAUL CHITLIK

Legendary screenwriting instructor and award-winning writer Paul Chitlik presents an easy-to-read, step-by-step process to take your script from first draft to submission draft. He reveals the hidden structure of screenplays, sequences, and scenes, as he guides you through the process of examining your draft, restructuring it, and populating it with believable, complex, and compelling characters.

Along the way he outlines how to make your action leap off the page and your dialogue crackle. While the first edition was widely used in film school rewriting classes, it was also recommended as an introduction to screenwriting craft by a number of professors and professionals. Paul Chitlik has included, for the second edition, more examples, exercises, and applications for television, the web, and other media, using a wide range of citations in film, television, and the Internet to underline his approach.

"Whether you're an expert, journeyman, or beginner, Rewrite *will smooth and improve the way you revise your scripts."*

– Jody Wheeler, writer and director, *The Dark Place*; producer, *Judas Kiss*

"Paul has forgotten more about the art of writing than most people ever know. This book is a wealth of information for the writer going it alone."

– Joel Zwick, director, *My Big Fat Greek Wedding*

PAUL CHITLIK has written for all the major networks and studios in English and in Spanish. He was story editor for MGM/UA'S "The New Twilight Zone," and staff writer for Showtime's sitcom "Brothers." He has written features for Rysher Entertainment, NuImage, Promark, Mainline Releasing, and others. He has directed episodes and been coordinating producer for "Real Stories of the Highway Patrol" and "U.S. Customs Classified." He wrote and produced "Alien Abduction," the first network movie shot on digital video for UPN. He wrote, produced, and directed "Ringling Brothers Revealed" a special for The Travel Channel. (He had been a roustabout for Circus Vargas years earlier.) Most recently he wrote, produced and directed "The Wedding Dress," for Amazon Prime. He received a Writers Guild of America award nomination for his work on "The Twilight Zone" and a GLAAD Media Award nomination for "Los Beltrán," a Telemundo show.

$17.21 · 124 PAGES · ISBN: 9781615931576

© Michele Montez

MICHAEL WIESE PRODUCTIONS

In a dark time, a light bringer came along, leading the curious and the frustrated to clarity and empowerment. It took the well-guarded secrets out of the hands of the few and made them available to all. It spread a spirit of openness and creative freedom, and built a storehouse of knowledge dedicated to the betterment of the arts.

The essence of Michael Wiese Productions (MWP) is empowering people who have the burning desire to express themselves creatively. We help them realize their dreams by putting the tools in their hands. We demystify the sometimes secretive worlds of screenwriting, directing, acting, producing, film financing, and other media crafts.

By doing so, we hope to bring forth a realization of 'conscious media,' which we define as being positively charged, emphasizing hope, and affirming positive values like trust, cooperation, self-empowerment, freedom, and love. Grounded in the deep roots of myth, it aims to be healing both for those who make the art and those who encounter it. It hopes to be transformative for people, opening doors to new possibilities and pulling back veils to reveal hidden worlds.

MWP has built a storehouse of knowledge unequaled in the world, for no other publisher has so many titles on the media arts. Please visit www.mwp.com, where you will find many free resources and a 25% discount on our books. Sign up and become part of the wider creative community!

Michael Wiese, Co-Publisher
Geraldine Overton, Co-Publisher